AURAL HABILITATION

AURAL

HABILITATION

A Total Approach

By

R. E. HARTBAUER, Ph.D.

Associate Professor, Audiology/Speech Pathology
Marquette University
Milwaukee, Wisconsin
Associate Clinical Professor of Otolaryngology
Medical College of Wisconsin
Milwaukee, Wisconsin
Chief of Audiology, Department of Otolaryngology
Veterans Administration Center
Wood (Milwaukee), Wisconsin

CHARLES C THOMAS · PUBLISHER
Springfield · Illinois · U.S.A.

Published and Distributed Throughout the World by
CHARLES C THOMAS • PUBLISHER
BANNERSTONE HOUSE
301-327 East Lawrence Avenue, Springfield, Illinois, U.S.A.

© *1975, by* CHARLES C THOMAS • PUBLISHER
ISBN 0-398-03040-5
Library of Congress Catalog Card Number: 73-17027

With THOMAS BOOKS *careful attention is given to all details of manufacturing and design. It is the Publisher's desire to present books that are satisfactory as to their physical qualities and artistic possibilities and appropriate for their particular use.* THOMAS BOOKS *will be true to those laws of quality that assure a good name and good will.*

Printed in the United States of America
N-1

Library of Congress Cataloging in Publication Data

Hartbauer, R. E.
    Aural habilitation; a total approach.

    Bibliography: p.
    1. Deaf—Education. 2. Deaf—Means of communication. I. Title.
[DNLM: 1. Hearing aids. 2. Hearing disorders—Rehabilitation. WV270
H326a 1973]
HV2430.H37   371.9'12   73-17027
ISBN 0-398-03040-5

Dedicated To
The deaf who teach me to listen and hear.

INTRODUCTION

I N THIS AGE OF ELECTICISM, this book is designed to stimulate a discussion of the problems involved in aural habilitation and rehabilitation. The text is designed for reading by persons having their first exposure to the problems of the hearing handicapped. These would be college students in introductory courses, parents of hearing impaired children and counsellors in allied fields. It is designed to serve as an introduction to the problems of the hearing impaired and to give some direction to helping them in learning the communication process.

In several places in the book there are statements made which may seem radical or even untrue by persons of a particular school of thought. They are, however, the feelings, experiences and attitudes of persons with other orientations and have been gleaned from countless hours of conversation with adult deaf who have been taught with all the methods. The text handles four basic concerns: the psychological and social aspects of an aural dysfunction; the use of electronic amplification; the total use of the visual *back-up* system, that is, aural and manual; and the teaching of concepts as the primary method of training.

The author is aware that a text should encourage more questions than it answers just as good teaching *forces* the superior student to search beyond the basic requirements of the course. It is hoped that this book will give the reader direction to follow in searching for those answers.

CONTENTS

AURAL HABILITATION

CHAPTER 1

THE HEARING IMPAIRED

SEVERAL PHILOSOPHERS have stated that a measure of a society's civilization is the manner in which it treats the exceptional segment of its population. Throughout the ages the deaf have been considered saints or demons, gifted or deprived. They have been shunned, mocked, tortured, ridiculed, and exiled. The deaf have been considered demented, criminal, mean, or retarded. Such reactions to this part of the world's population was due largely to ignorance and an unwillingness on the part of both the *learned and ordinary man* to investigate the true nature of the hearing impairment and its companion involvements. By and large, in this age of enlightenment these reactions have changed to a searching for a compliant understanding of this sensory deprivation and an acceptance of such an afflicted person as a worthy human being. It can be said, therefore, that with our more intelligent handling of these persons we are a more civilized society.

History records that a statement of the philosopher, Aristotle, was misconstrued and his comment about the deaf resulted in the belief that though the deaf had voice, speechlessness meant that the deaf did not have the mental capacity to learn speech.

Biblical references noted, on the other hand, that the Hebrew nations were instructed, "Thou shalt not curse the deaf." (Lev. 19:14). And, in another reference it is recorded they were to "Bring forth the blind people that have eyes and the deaf that have ears" (Isa. 43:8) as a way of declaring they were educable.

During the dark ages the deaf were included in the array of deformed and handicapped used as court jesters and as the butts of humor. This basically was the prevailing attention given them until the 1500's. Jerome Cardan, an Italian physician, was willing to declare and demonstrate that the deaf had the organs necessary

3

for speech and could be taught to use them. It was during this time that Pedro Ponce de Leon, by his belief that the deaf could be taught to speak and be taught academically, became the first modern teacher of the deaf. With the impetus from his success, the training of the deaf led to the educational concerns we have today. Both the oral and manual methods were used. Some of the teachers had greater success with one or the other. In either case, the teachers were more concerned with the deaf person's learning than in defending his teachings.

It is agreed that the first text on the use of lip-reading as the pedagogical procedure was written in 1620 by Juan Pablo Bonet. His belief was that even though not everyone could be taught to lip-read, certain individuals could at least be taught to lip-read their teachers. He doubted that their lip-reading ability could carry over to reading other persons' lips.

In 1648, John Bulwar, in England, was enthusiastic about extending the use of lipreading beyond the deaf person's academic learning from this technique to using it as a means of helping the deaf learn to speak. It can be said, then, that he was the forerunner of those who attempted speech in the deaf.

Delgarno, in Scotland, believed that the deaf did not learn so much by lipreading and the movements of the lips, but understood as a result of such things as time, place, person, etc. He scorned the use of lipreading and speech and employed the usage of letters of the alphabet on the palms and fingertips of the hand whereon messages were spelled. A similar glove was used later, in America, by Alexander Graham Bell.

In 1687, a Swiss physician, Amman, stated his belief that the muteness accompanying deafness is caused by the deafness. He extensively used mirror practice for teaching both speech and lipreading.

Following success in teaching a young deaf girl, Henry Baker, in 1720, began a small private school in England. The tragedy of the history is that he would not reveal his techniques and procedures. Some writers speculate that his being a naturalist played a unique and fascinating role.

Both lipreading and the manual alphabet were taught by

Jacob R. Periere, a Spaniard, working in France. He can be considered a forefather of the total communication emphasis. He differed from Baker in that Baker refused to record his methods while Periere neglected to do so.

Another forefather of total communication was Charles de l'Epee in Paris. He was also the founder of the first public school for the aurally handicapped. It was established in Vienna in 1799, and was directed, after the death of de l'Epee, by Sicard. The emphasis of de l'Epee was on integrating the deaf into society by teaching them speech and lipreading, but the great number of students forced him to use signing, also.

During the same period, the oral school was gaining emphasis by the teaching of Samuel Heinicke, in Germany. Believing that clear thinking was possible for the deaf only if they speak, he stressed oralism. He further believed that lipreading was the method for learning how to understand speech.

Thomas Braidwood, in Great Britain, who, believing the deaf heard with their eyes, used the lipreading system. Francis Green, the father of one of Braidwood's students, Charles Green, advocated public schooling for the deaf in both the old and new countries. Braidwood's work did not cease with his death but was continued by his widow, his son, and eventually by his son's widow. His grandson, John Braidwood, upon immigrating to America, established a school sponsored by a Virginian in 1815.

At the safe time, a minister named Thomas Gallaudet studied in England at the Braidwood institution. While he was there he learned of the successes of Sicard, in France, employing the manual procedure.

Gallaudet persuaded Laurent Clerc, a deaf teacher, to come from France to America, and they established the American Asylum for the Deaf, which was later named the American School for the Deaf.

Another European traveler, Horace Mann, returned to America. With a $50,000 contribution from John Clarke he began an oral school in Northampton, Massachusetts in 1867. A second oral school was started in Boston two years later.

In the Boston school, Alexander Graham Bell instructed with

the Visible Speech Symbols that had been conceived by his father, Melville Bell.

There were several publications regarding the deaf during these years. At the Hartford school the *American Annals of the Deaf and Dumb* was published in 1847 by the Convention of the American Instructors of the Deaf and Dumb. In 1899, the fore-runner of the *Volta Review* was issued under the name *Association Review*.

Up to this time, the 1890's, teaching of the deaf was limited to children, but Lillie Warren and her assistant, Edward Nichie, taught adults. They believed that there were sixteen facial con-figurations which showed the sounds of English speech. Their approach was called the numerical cipher method.

In contrast to the analytical approach, at the 1894 Conference of the American Association, Mrs. Alexander Graham Bell urged a synthetic approach to promote the teaching of speech to the deaf. She believed the emphasis should be on the ability of the deaf to grasp the meaning the speaker was conveying rather than on understanding each word or sentence. Her deafness qualified her to speak with experience rather than just being an advocate of a particular school of thought.

Since the turn of the century, America has seen many advo-cates of particular approaches. After her studying in Germany, under Herr Mueller-Walle, Martha Bruhn founded a school in America in 1902, with close observation of lip movements and much syllable drill.

Edward Mitchie, a student under Lillie Warren, later opened a school, in 1903, which taught regular school subjects to deaf children and in time shifted to education of adult deaf. As he strived to improve his procedures, he changed from a strictly ana-lytical to a synthetic school of thought. His wife continued his school after his untimely death at age forty.

In 1914, Cora Kinzie began the Mueller-Walle School of Lip-reading in Philadelphia. Her sister, Rose, joined her six years later and they devoted all their time to the development of graded lessons in lipreading. Series I through III were for children, IV for adult beginners and V through VIII were for advanced lip-readers, usually adults.

In the early 1900's, Anna Bunger contributed to the American deaf education by advocating what is called the Jena method. Bunger had studied the method of Karl Brauchmann in Jena, Germany. Its unique feature was the emphasis on using visual and kinesthetic cues. Many feel today that this is one of the more scientifically based approaches.

With the advent of the motion picture industry, Marie Mason developed film techniques for teaching the hearing deprived during the 1930's and early 1940's. During the late 1940's Boris Morkovin and Lucelia Moore, at the University of Southern California, developed life situation films for teaching lipreading.

In the 1960's and 1970's video tape recording has become economically feasible to most clinics and centers. The virtue of using it is still being evaluated. Research into new ideas, techniques, and procedures goes on while the values of oral, manual, and total schools continue to be debated. As long as there is still controversy there will be continued investigation into improved ways to teach the deaf and hard of hearing within our society.

CLASSIFICATION OF HEARING LEVELS

In our study of the hearing impaired, the word *deaf* is used in many ways.

In one context, the term *deaf* can refer to anyone who does not possess what is considered normal hearing. This is the usual connotation when there is a discussion of children in school settings. It is the connotation to the man on the street who has no knowledge of a variety of hearing defects, and when a final definitive diagnosis is pending.

The next reference contrasts deaf and deafened. The former is the person who has been deprived of his hearing prior to the acquisition of his speech communication arts and skills. This individual is the one who has congenital sensory deprivation from hereditary factors, maternal rubella during the first trimester of the pregnancy, intrauteral toxins and antitoxins, Rh factor (blood incompatibility), premature birth, anoxia at birth (lack of oxygen), trauma at birth, and congenital malformation of the ear. There is currently ongoing research into the effects on the hearing of the fetus with drugs such as heroin and marijuana. Reports indicate significant toxicity, but with such variability that it is difficult to show a pattern.

If the child is born with normal hearing there are numerous causes of subsequent hearing loss. Primate offenders are measles, mumps, whooping cough, scarlet fever, meningitis, and other diseases accompanied by a prolonged high fever.

Hearing can also be affected by ear trauma and ear infections. The ear trauma is caused by the entrance of objects into the ear canal, such as sticks, pencils, sharp fingernails or buttons. It is too easy to inadvertently destroy the canal wall tissue or the tympanic membrane (eardrum). Even though the membrane may heal, there is the risk of ossicular disruption or permanent scar tissue formation in the middle ear.

Frequently diseases are due to unhygenic conditions and poor personal grooming which permit bacterial growth. Improper care during common colds may result in the invasion of bacterias and viruses through the eustachian tube into the middle ear cavity. In some of the tropical countries, fungus infections may also occur.

An infant may be given medications which precipitate hearing loss. Occasionally there are hearing losses due to blows on the head such as from auto accidents or child abuse.

Any one or any combination of these etiologic factors may deprive the child of his hearing before he learns his speech communication, probably before the age of four years. Continued education of the parents and improved and expanded neonate screening will aid in early detection, observation and definitive therapy.

The deafened are all those persons who acquire hearing impairments after they have learned the communication systems. Nearly all of the postnatal causes of loss can be etiologically connected to the deafened. With no attempt to be exhaustive in the listing of possible causes, we include toxicity by drugs and medications, skin diving, blows on the head, acoustic trauma as in industry or the intensity of most rock and roll bands, venereal disease (primarily syphilis), war injuries and the aging process.

The loss may be transitory if it is of a conductive type and can be treated medically and/or surgically. Yet, even with appropriate therapy there can be a residual loss.

Next, let us consider deaf-hard of hearing. A rather standard classifying of the hearing level follows: 0-25dB through the speech range frequencies, 500-2000 Hz, the individual is considered to have hearing within normal limits. There can be sensori-neural losses that are not demonstrated by pure tone and speech testing data within the 0-25dB range. Advanced otological and audiological diagnostic procedures are employed when clinical observations suspect this diagnosis.

Hearing levels 30-45dB are mild losses, 45-60dB are moderate, 60-80dB severe, and more than 80dB are profound. Depending on the school of thought, the latter are considered either profoundly hard of hearing or deaf. The alternate school says that the patients should not be considered deaf unless the loss is sufficient to prevent usable hearing, even with amplification.

Alternatives to the connotations and denotations of *deaf* will be kept in mind.

Medically and legally, the aural habilitation team is asked to determine the percentage of hearing loss. Industrial compensation needs a reference point and a way of relating to that reference point, and a percentage scale serves that purpose. Most scales are at least based on the criteria established by the Academy of Ophthalmology and Otolaryngology of the American Medical Association. The criteria vary from state to state, and in some instances from interest to interest such as insurance companies. The best advice is to recommend the current standards from the local or state medical society office.

Gradually, within the last few years, thoughts have been directed toward hearing levels, hearing functions, residual hearing rather than the degree of loss. Positive thinking is part of total rehabilitation.

PSYCHOLOGICAL ASPECTS

The next part of the discussion is devoted to generalities written by teachers of the deaf, counsellors of the deaf and, most importantly, by the deaf. They are not universally true but significant enough to be given critical consideration.

1.   More emotional problems may develop in the deaf than in the hearing child.
2.   Deaf, and primarily the deafened, may develop feelings of insecurity and become paranoidal.
3.   The deafened may lose interest in social activities.
4.   Women, more than men, develop feelings of isolation.
5.   Hearing impaired children suffer more ridicule because of their speech than because of the hearing problem.
6.   Any language deficiency is not due to lack of intelligence or psychopathology.
7.   They may develop dependency relationships that are not healthy.
8.   A basic fear regarding marriage is that they may have deaf children.
9.   Some deaf children tend to be aggressive.
10.   Hard of hearing individuals must exert extra effort to meet the demands of adjustment to a hearing world.

Two critical considerations in the psychological consequence of hearing deprivation are age of onset and the level of hearing. An early onset can be either a positive or negative factor. Evidence indicates that some families are more likely to adjust to an early onset rather than a later one. The child needs to find an identify. The family creates that identity by the manner in which the child is treated, both before and after the assessment of hearing privation.

Identification refers to the feelings and attitudes of the individual toward himself and how he relates that *self* to others. For example, does he view himself as a healthy, normal, whole person who happens to have a hearing loss? Or, does he view himself as a grotesque hearing loss? Does he see himself as an individual with a normal capacity to think and reason, or does he question whether or not he thinks the same way others do? Does he ask himself if he has the same kind of brain that hearing people have? Does he internalize and feel that it is all his fault and does not know that part of the problem is the inability of others to understand and accept? What does he see in the mirror? What does he see and who does he see when he reads what he has written?

What about isolation? Hearing is a distance sense perceptor. The total aural habilitation team has to give that deaf person proximity to himself and to others. We must help that person see a healthy, vigorous person with potentials to be discovered and developed. Take, for example, the needs of deaf people during the dining hours. It can be a shattering experience, leaving one quite alone in a group. While eating, the normal hearing gives little thought to sign language or lipreading. Have you ever tried to lip-read someone whose mouth is filled.

Extroversion-introversion, dominant, retiring, aggression, competitiveness, sources of security and stability, rigidity of behavior, and male-female identity are prime considerations to the deaf and deafened.

For the sake of illustration of a psycho-socio-emotional part of life, it is said that deaf have more sexual problems. It is not that they are more promiscuous, but they do not understand many of the ramifications of the sexual aspects of life. Usually their associates have not deemed it essential to teach them. As one deaf adult recently told the writer, "People assume that because we are deaf we have no sex identity, no sex drives, and therefore no healthy inquiry and no need to know. Why can't people understand that deafness doesn't affect the rest of our bodies?"

Do the deaf have feelings of rejection? They do because they sense the truth. The community, the culture, the society, and the world are related to these segments of our population. The rest of us, too, have basic needs to help us relate to the deaf.

First, there must be an acceptance of deafness. There must be the acceptance that it is a reality. The deaf individual must be accepted. The person wants, first of all, acceptance. He does not want approval or disapproval. It would be just as pathological for a person to say "Doctor, I want you to approve of my having pneumonia," rather than saying "what can be done about it?" Or, how foolish it would be for someone to say, "I disapprove of your being blind."

After the acceptance of reality, which goes hand in hand with the understanding of it, habilitation proceeds. Total acceptance incorporates a willingness, perhaps even an eagerness, to move forward. There is a vast desolation of ignorance, and understanding compels people to move on.

A part of acceptance of the deaf is acceptance of self by each member of the constellation. Accept and understand self and your own idiosyncrasies will not be inflicted on the hearing deprived. Each one must ask, "How do I react to deaf people? What does it do to me? Why do I feel uncomfortable around them?" "Why am I on this habilitation team? What more can I do?" In summary, an intelligent, healthy image of self will result in a more intelligent and healthy image of the auditorily sensory deprived.

CHAPTER 2

THE SENSE MODALITIES – VISION AND HEARING

S CIENTIFIC RESEARCH has a concern over limits of variables. The investigators are concerned over how much, how many, which and how long. They pose their hypotheses on the concern of limits. Regardless of the ultimate design, they are interested in the thresholds of their subjects or materials. Only after they know the thresholds can they measure the amount of suprathreshold stimuli they are employing.

By definition, threshold is the least amount of stimulus needed to elicit a response 50 percent of the time. It is based in physiological research, on the premise that, at threshold, nerve fibers fire half of the time in response to stimuli. This is true of the sense modalities for both threshold of awareness, toleration or pain. By thus setting both thresholds we establish the range within which the senses function.

There are also thresholds for just noticeable differences when employing suprathreshold stimuli. Many researchers equate the J.N.D. (just noticeable difference) test with the difference limen tests. In these tests, two stimuli of identical characteristics are presented, and then one is varied under stringent control until the subject signals that he is aware that the two are no longer identical. Both the normal and the abnormal sense modalities may have some difficulty differentiating between stimuli. On the other hand, the abnormal may be sensitive to minimal differences.

It is imperative that a threshold be established for the person's hearing ability, both for determining the amount of residual hearing and for a reference to monitor any possible change. The audiogram is a record of how the person responded to sounds at a certain time under certain conditions. Intelligent interpreters of audiograms are cognizant of the fact that this either may or may not be an indication of the person's true hearing threshold.

The audiogram is also a record of the competency of the tester. There is a constant monitoring and upgrading of audiologists by the American Board of Examiners in Speech Pathology and Audiology of the American Speech and Hearing Association and by its Committee on Clinical Certification.

Audiograms are records of the threshold values for the octave pure tone sounds, 125—8000 Hz. The configurations of the threshold readings indicate the type and extent of hearing loss or the hearing level. Thresholds for both air condition and bone condition testing are needed for basic interpretation to ascertain the classification of involvement (loss) and, thus, to determine whether or not the problem may be resolved by medical and/or surgical procedures.

Next, the person is administered a speech reception threshold test which indicates the intensity level needed for the subject to identify 50 percent of the words given to him under controlled conditions, either by monitored live voice or recorded voice. Frequently, an additional speech threshold is given whereby the person merely indicates his awareness of the presence of speech sounds but is unable to interpret the words. There is a several decible difference between this detection threshold (D.T.) and the speech reception threshold (S.R.T.).

SUPRATHRESHOLD PERCEPTION

Many testing techniques can be used by the audiologist including ascending, descending and automatic. Regardless of the one used, the findings become the reference point for suprathreshold testing. Basically, suprathreshold investigation determines how the subject functions when the stimuli are presented with sufficient intensity for the subject not to be concerned over presence or non-presence of the stimulus. Suprathreshold testing determines how the subject functions in relation to *normals* or to others with similar abnormalities. In auditory testing, it indicates how the person performs with electronic amplification.

Several suprathreshold tests aid in what is called *site of lesion* testing. They help isolate the particular part of the auditory mechanism that is affected. Knowledge of the site of the lesion is critical to therapy and in the planning of post-testing programs, i.e. auditory training, visual training, medical follow-up and counseling.

The most critical auditory suprathreshold test is the discrimination test for speech. As a result of research done by the Bell Telephone Company, the Harvard Psycho-Acoustics Laboratories, the Central Institute for the Deaf and others, lists of words each have been created that theoretically contain all the speech sounds found in common American English with approximately the usual ratio of words for each list. Both adult and children's lists exist. They are called *phonetically balanced* words. We find a myriad of terms used in referring to the results. The common terms are discrimination Scores, PB Scores and PB Max (imum) Scores. Just as with the Speech Reception Threshold Tests, these tests can be administered by either recorded or monitored live voice. A high score means that the person has little trouble in understanding speech when it is comfortably above his threshold.

SENSORY DEPRIVATION

Time of onset of loss may be as significant as the amount and type of loss. The time of onset of hearing loss places the habilitation personnel at different starting points for the different types of losses. Each hearing impaired person has his own unique experiential or referential backlog to call upon.

Hearing losses should not be considered as all or none entities. Most states and organizations declare that the total loss of one ear does not mean that the person loses half of his hearing, but that he loses 1/5 to 1/8 (depending on the criteria). Nor is the same amount of hearing loss for different frequencies the same. Lower frequency losses are considered more significant. These factors are based on the assumption that the understanding of speech is the paramount need. Usually in medico-legal cases the level of only the 500, 1000 and 2000Hz pure tone thresholds are considered. No concern is given to the other total speech range frequencies from 125-6000 Hz.

The deafened have known life with normal hearing and the loss of hearing is taking away something upon which they have learned to depend. That deprivation must be assessed. Upon that assessment we build habilitation and rehabilitation programs.

SENSORY DISTORTION

A partial hearing impairment can be just as complicating and bewildering as a total loss of hearing. A popular television program has, as part of its design, the showing of parts of a picture message one part at a time until there are enough clues visible for one of the contestants to interpret the pieces of symbols correctly. Think of the utter frustration if the technician running the display board were to never reveal those last few essential parts. This is analogous to the person with partial hearing. Another way of demonstrating this distortion would be to block out all the letters on this page which stand for high frequency sounds (v, f, z, s, θ, t, th, *th*) and then set out to read it for the first time. The reader would find this a most trying task.

In these two analogies, we referred to the sensory distortion present in some sounds and absent in others; that is, distortion by partial, selective elimination of sound. This results in the hearing impaired person not hearing some sounds, like the (s), that has high frequency ˏfundamental acoustic components, or the missing of some critical high frequency components of other sounds, like the (th), that has low frequency fundamental acoustic power. There is some difference in the two situations, in that, with the high frequency harmonics loss, there is at least some hint of what the sound is like.

Yet another type of sensory distortion exists. In cochlear disease, with destruction of hair cells, the sounds may be loud enough for the person to hear but there is restricted capacity to clearly understand and differentiate among similar sounds. The tone deaf person is unable to tell if two or more sounds are the same or different in frequency. He cannot identify sounds of different pitches just as the individual with a cochlear pathology cannot identity differences of speech sounds.

In some instances, there is actually a reception of alternate and/or spurious sounds known as diplacusis. In other instances, the person has difficulty in hearing noise. He may need a better signal to noise ratio. Any hearing function that allows the sound to reach the cortex of the listener without clarity is an instance of hearing sensory distortion.

SENSE MODALITY COMPENSATORY ACTIVITY

There is another type of compensatory functioning, that of the blind person. He relies more on his other senses. He trains, until it becomes reflex to listen more critically and to feel more discriminatively. He is using sensory compensatory activities.

In the same manner, the deaf or deafened must rely on alternate avenues of communication. If he cannot hear he is faced with the urgency of using his vision as the second best modality. The hearing handicapped also develop a greater sensitivity to touch. The kinesthetic circuit is tuned and, in many individuals, the senses of smell and taste are more acute.

In aural habilitation, vision is usually the receptive sense that is trained. We are trying to increase the ability of the deaf to rely on what he sees, to discriminate among similarities, to interpret what he sees, to use what he obtains from vision to develop his own expressive powers. His eyes are compensating for his ears, but they are not substituting for them. How absurd it would be to say that a person can hear the hues of a rainbow or hear a frown or smile. True, there may be accompanying noises with the latter but it still remains he could not hear either one. With sight compensation for vision, a person cannot see inflections and pitch in the spoken word. He cannot see the melody of a song. The role of the habilitation therapist is to help the deaf observe alternate signs and symbols to understand and produce the inflections, pitches and melodies of speech. Facial expressions, gesturing signs, markings on the chalkboard, arrows, darts and lines are used. Positions and motions are also used. All the programs are designed to help the deaf use vision to compensate for the hearing impairment as he communicates.

THE MULTIPLE HANDICAPPED

In the child or adult who has been deprived of both normal hearing and normal vision, there must initially be a determination of the lesser handicap. Should he be considered a deaf-blind person or a blind-deaf person. Historically, teacher training programs have concentrated on the deaf-blind, implying that the blindness is the greater affliction.

Assuming the blindness is the greater impairment, the habilitation program must rely on the residual hearing. Auditory training, usually with electronic amplification, is the channel. Lesson plans have the audition assisting the residual vision and the education process capitalizes on the remaining hearing.

When the greater affliction is deprivation of hearing, the lesson plans and the educational emphasis is on the maximum use of the residual vision to help train any remaining hearing.

In the vision *and* hearing impaired the other senses come into play even more dynamically. The sensation of touch becomes acute. Possibly the most dramatic instance of modern time is that of Helen Keller who learned by way of touch and finger spelling on her hands. Her teacher had an arduous task which ended in phenomenal success.

Aural habilitation specialists realize that there are five senses (sight, smell, touch, taste, hear) which function, both individually and in harmony with each other. Aural habilitation in this context, too, falls short if there is not a total approach.

CHAPTER 3

ELECTRONIC AMPLIFICATION

AFTER THE CENTURIES during which the deaf (hearing impaired) were relegated to the role of being minimally educable they have arrived at a status within our society where they are considered no more uneducable than persons with other abnormal characteristics. Today that image is being improved. Within the last few years audiologists working with this population have begun to refer to hearing levels rather than hearing losses. The emphasis is on what the person has at his disposal, not on what he never had or has lost. When the remaining hearing is considered, there is direction and guidance for utilization after the audiological evaluation.

In this chapter, the discussion will be on how to assist the partially handicapped to hear. No audiologist would consider trying to get sound into a totally deaf ear. There are people with no usable residual hearing.

Audiologists often see patients who claim they can hear as well as ever, but that everyone else is beginning to mumble. There are parents who do not understand the complexity of a partial hearing loss and declare, "But my child hears and listens if I raise my voice to him." On the other hand, there are those who have only a minimal amount of hearing low frequency sounds presented at great intensity. These people may or may not know they are handicapped.

With wild or maximal deprivation, individuals will possibly benefit from amplified sounds. Amplification is not a perfect entity. It cannot fully resolve the hearing deficit. Conscientious hearing aid dealers stress this point. Hearing aids only make the sound louder, as modified by the circuitry. The audiologist and hearing aid dealer critically interpret the audiometric data to determine which type of hearing aid has the best characteristics for the patient. They ascertain: How much amplification is needed, and how little and how much can he get by with? Is there proper selective amplification of some sounds? Does the person need amplification on one or both ears? Are the audiograms similar for the two ears? Can the individual manipulate the controls on the instrument himself with ease? Does the person need sufficient amplification to justify recommending a body type rather than an ear level aid? The body type aid can provide more power than the others. The needs of a child of preschool years, a younger person in an integrated classroom, a businessman, or a senior citizen are vastly different.

The results obtained with amplification are also individual. The writer recalls two illustrative incidents regarding the use of amplification. The first was when a 29-year-old mother heard her own *baby's low cry* for the first time. The other is that of a 62-year-old man who returned just to say, "I can hear the calls now when my girlfriend and I go square dancing."

There are many psychological and social problems facing the hearing aid user. Both young and old may resent the invasion of sound into their silent worlds. Primarily, this is because the sounds they hear through the hearing aid appear distorted. The person is not aware that the aid amplifies all sounds and may feel confused or bewildered when the signals he wants to hear are not the only ones that are louder. The younger person may be hearing sounds for the first time and the sounds have no meaning. An analogy may be that of hearing the words of a foreign language for the first time. If sounds do not have any value, they are considered to be noise and attempts are made to ignore them. Many times, when aids are placed on infants, the problem of resenting sound does not exist because the child develops hearing with the instrument, orientation to sound and language simultaneously.

The elderly may resent an aid because: First, that wearing an aid is a big flag saying *I'm falling apart.* It is not as socially acceptable as eyeglasses. Second, aging persons may feel that they have heard as much as they have wanted and now wish to live in relative silence.

When the audiologist or hearing aid dealer is counseling elderly people it is important to stress the point that, *using a hearing aid will make it easier for others to communicate with an individual.* This idea is usually a convincing point with senior citizens who want to communicate with their loved ones.

The hearing habilitation team frequently must make difficult decisions. When working with one type of patient there may be a need to discourage the use of a hearing aid. The new user must be aware of the limits of an aid and must realize that it will not be as effective as normal hearing in many situations. He must know that it is in many ways *inconvenient* and demands *maintenance.* The hearing habilitation team member should try to evaluate what, where and why the person *wants* to hear and what he *needs* to hear.

In the hearing aid evaluation procedure, there are several routines used in selecting the aid. The patient may declare, *"That one sounds the best to me,"* when the audiometric data reveal otherwise. The brand X that he prefers may not be helping him; that is, it may not be amplifying sound adequately. It may actually be permitting him to hear essentially as he has been hearing, while another aid which he does not prefer may be giving him better discrimination of sounds. An experienced hearing aid user may want a new one to sound *just like mine,* when it may be that another instrument would be better for him.

These problems exist to a lesser degree with younger children. They tend to be perceptive and more receptive to the interpretation of the test data.

The ultimate goal is selection of the amplification which results in the best discrimination of sounds in numerous everyday environments. Beyond the selection of the basic instrument there is much refinement of the sound by the judicial consideration of tubing, filters and ear molds, and adjustments of the hearing aid's response curve and output.

During the evaluation and after the selection there must be an orientation to the use of the device. A typical series of thoughts presented are:

1. Remember, this does *not* give you normal hearing.

2. Allow yourself three to eight weeks before expecting maximum benefit.

3. Use the aid daily for as long as you can easily tolerate it. The tolerance period will become longer and longer.

4. Get reacquainted (or acquainted) with sounds like the rattling of dishes, rustle of paper, click of your heels, the doorbell and the telephone, coughing, and clothing noises.

5. Try it out in a one to one conversation in a quiet setting until you have mastered it quite well.

6. Next, get involved in small group conversations with some background noises such as a radio, television, or children.

7. Go out into the work-a-day world and try it out. You will find the street noises are a complicating thing at first, particularly if you have not religiously followed the above listed steps.

8. Return to this office for routine followup to discuss any problems with the aid or adjustment to using it.

When an aid is placed on a child who has a severe auditory deprivation, not having heard unamplified sound, the first step is to help him learn what the sounds are. He must be *convinced* that sound has meaning and purpose, and then when he understands what it is he can use the same sounds and mold his environment. He must be taught that sound is a tool that both he and others use to communicate with one another. Gradually he is to be guided from the interpretation of gross sounds to the point where he can find meaning and use in the finer discrimination among sounds. Gradually he hears others using speech sounds and incorporates them into his own auditory memory and vocabulary. This is a time consuming and tedious process that lasts for as long as the child is receiving his formal training.

The availability of service for hearing aids is important. Consideration should be given to the ease with which the instrument can be repaired or adjusted. It would be sensible to purchase the aid closer to the home or place of employment rather than in some remote part of town, or from a dealer who does not have an established place of business.

HEARING AIDS

There are basic components and functions of an aid which are essential. First, there is a microphone. Regardless of its type (ceramic, crystal, electronic), its function is to receive airborne sound waves and transduce those compressions and rarifactions of air molecules into electronic impulses. The characteristics and abilities of the microphone extensively influence which sounds will be amplified. The newer microphones determine, in part, not only which frequencies will be translated but from which direction the sounds will be retrieved. One way this is done is by controlling the phase relationship of the sounds coming from various directions.

The size of the microphone has limited the range of frequencies in transducers. New microphones are permitting further subminiaturization while extending the range. Possibly this may be a breakthrough for amplifying sounds of the entire speech range.

When the sound has become electronic energy it enters the amplifier. Transistorizing of aids has let the industry miniaturize more than the tube amplifiers. Transistors have a more stable sound. Within the amplifier, the resistors and condensors and other components influence which type and intensity of sound will be amplified. One aid will give what is called *flat* response, with all frequencies amplified equally. This type of aid is used by a person with a conductive or unusual sensori-neural loss. Another aid for a person with a marked loss of high frequencies will have a circuitory called *high pass,* with the electronic components suppressing the low frequencies and letting high frequencies pass.

After the electronic energy has been modified and increased by the amplification, it passes into the receiver. The receiver has the same function as a speaker in a public address system—it takes the amplified electronic energy and reverses the process of the microphone. It transduces the energy back into airborne compressions and rarifactions which we call *sound.* Research on receivers has aided in the research on microphones, as has research on microphones aided in developing receivers. The elements in the receiver further influence the production of sound.

Another part of an aid is the ear mold, also called the ear-piece. Each person has a custom mold made from an impression taken of his auricle and outer ear canal. Comfort and acoustic effect determine the type of mold to be used. Many audiologists and teachers of the deaf leave the type of ear mold to the discretion of the dispensing hearing aid dealer.

Several of the controls and adjustments are permanently set, but others are variable with the discretion of the wearer. The range of frequencies, how high and how low, is set by the circuitry. The Hearing Aid Industry Conference has established criteria to be used in evaluating the function of aids. Using these criteria, the manufacturers can declare the peak gain of the aid; that is, the greatest amount of amplification provided by the most increased frequency; the average gain, which is the amount of amplification provided, as calculated by three standard frequencies; the maximum output; and the intensity of sound the instrument will deliver.

Most aids have volume controls which can be adjusted (by the wearer) to the maximum comfort loudness, and some have response curve selector switches. Others have telephone switches which pick up telephone sounds from a telephone receiver rather than through the microphone.

All members of the aural habilitation team must become acquainted with the hearing aid (s) worn by their patients.

AUDITORY TRAINERS

Nearly all institutions that train the hearing impaired have amplification systems that are of better fidelity than the wearable hearing aid. These larger units usually have wider ranges throughout the speech range of 125–6000 Hz and sometimes through 8000 Hz. Auditory trainers are worn by the students during their classroom hours. Teachers usually wear microphones and, in some programs, there is a microphone for each child in the room. With a multiplicity of microphones the children can efficiently hear each other as well as hearing the teacher. In other instances, the teacher has stereo microphones, and the auditory trainers deliver the sound through the headphones in true ster-

eophonic sound. Most systems merely deliver the sound binaur-
ally, but not in stereo, and the teacher wears earphones as does
each child.

During the early years of amplified training of the hearing
handicapped, all systems were tethered. There were outlets into
which the child plugged the cords for his headset. This limited
the range of movement. He had to unplug and then replug when
he went to another part of the room.

Another method of amplification with hearing aids involves
the teacher using a microphone, in which case the sound is amplified into the room to be picked up by the hearing aids. Feedback limits the range of movement by the teacher and also eliminates mircrophones for the students.

A major breakthrough in amplification for the deaf took place
with the development of the loop system. No longer was it necessary to have the umbilical tether. A wire loop is placed around
on the walls of the classroom and the amplified signal is broad-
cast through it. As long as the receiver is within that loop one
gets the benefit of the system. The microphones do not pick up
the signal. There is total freedom of movement within the room.

Next came the invention of frequency modulation (FM)
auditory trainers. The teacher has a transmitter, i.e. a subminia-
ture broadcasting station, and each child has a receiver. One company has developed a system of coded inserts which are frequency
selectors. Both the teacher and the child must have the same
coded insert for the system to function. FM auditory trainers can
be used on the playground for a considerable distance. And,
either in the classroom or on the playground, teachers on different frequencies can communicate with their own children.

Most systems are equipped with record players and radios.
All are designed to provide maximum flexibility and maximum
auditory experience.

CHAPTER 4

COMMUNICATION DEVELOPMENT FOR HEARING IMPAIRED

THE ULTIMATE GOAL in aural habilitation is for the hearing impaired subject to attain, as far as possible, the same communicative skills as those of the normal hearing individual. We will assume that he has no other deficits. We must, however, differentiate between the problems of the deaf and of the deafened.

First, let us attend to the problem of the deaf. These individuals live and grow with an experiential deficit. They do not have the pre-communication exposure or, at best, they have a distorted exposure because of their sensory deprivation. They do not have the input of meaningful sound; nor do they have the input of sound which makes non-acoustic stimuli meaningful. Without this input the profoundly deaf do not know that sounds exist. The severely hard of hearing do not get the full impact of the sound, they have a referential anemia. They do not have all the refereneces whereby stimuli can be interpreted into meaningful symbols. Things are of value or importance to a person when he can attach significance to them.

The normal hearing child has thousands of hours of exposure to speech and related sounds before he begins to develop his speech. The normal hearing child hears a specific word hundreds of times and in many references before it becomes his and he uses it meaningfully and correctly. Even this child may not have a perfect auditory picture of a speech sound (word) and may use another that may be only remotely related. If, however, that word is effective in modifying his environment, he will use it repeatedly because it has significance to him.

Persons not acquainted with the deaf become impatient when the deaf do not respond immediately with the *correct* word. They

26

do not realize this deficit exists.

Another analogy may be that of a normal hearing person hearing a term from a foreign language for the first time. The expression has no importance to him until he can put it into some type of setting. The hearer may note the surroundings, the speaker's actions or appearance, the voice and even the distractions. Then after he has taken these cues and has heard the same expression repeatedly will the expression become identifiable to correctly respond to and use.

The process of generalizing, a critical factor in acquiring communication skills, is the process whereby we relate one symbol to others of similar characteristics. It is the association of likes, likes with similarities and the differentiation of similarities. This is more difficult for the deaf because he does not have an auditory experiential or referential reservoir on which to rely. Therefore, it is our responsibility to find methods of helping the deaf relate sound symbols to meanings and sound symbols to other sound symbols. We also must help relate non-sound symbols (visual cues) to sound symbols and thus give them meaning.

The writer has noted that he and his associates have had the most success in teaching the deaf when concepts are employed. When a concept is the primary concern, the teacher is more effective in helping the deaf relate the sound symbols and meanings. The makeup of the teacher's lesson plan for language and concept development has more of what can be called "constructs".

CONSTRUCTS

The three general classifications of constructs are sequential, topical, and environmental.

Sequential Constructs. Students of languages are cognizant of the limitations inherent in any particular tongue. Each language has speech sounds which are more frequently used than are those sounds used in other languages. Various sounds found in some languages are omitted from others. An example is the /1/ not commonly found in the Japanese tongue. Another is the /ae/ which is not found in Spanish. In English, there is an absence of some sounds used by other nations or nationalities, and there are some combinations of sounds used that do not appear in our speech. We know, then, that the construct of the English language gives us direction and tells us that some possible sound combinations will not be probable. Thus, the sounds used in English and the accompanying English grammar is the sequential construct. If the words in a declarative sentence are rearranged, they can be formed into an interrogative sentence, still within the English sequential construct.

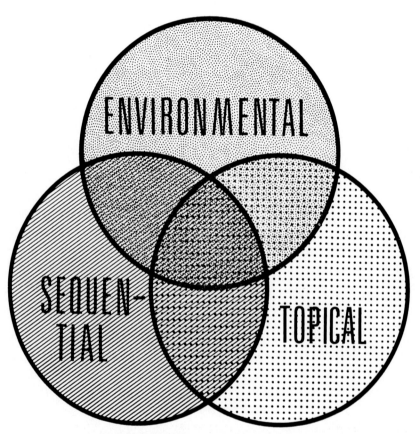

Figure 1. The functions of constructs are twofold: first they define the inclusive relevant characteristics and the common and pertinent aspects of environment sequence. Second, they are exclusive in that they rule out irrelevancies and nonessential alternatives. The three constructs are both independent and interactive. In most instances, each one influences the others.

The hearing impaired is taught that sequence is vital in the oral, manual, or total method. Not the position but the movement and progression of the articulators is stressed in lipreading. Just as true, the manual method stresses which sign is given first, which one second. The signing for verb tenses is the most dramatic. In most cases, the entire concept is changed with the re-sequencing of signs. Sequential constructs, peculiar to written English, are only alluded to, but our major interest is in spoken English for the deaf.

Topical Constructs. The person who acquires his hearing impairment prior to his acquisition of communication skills frequently has no auditory experience or recall. He has probably been limited to the present time and to the more tangible. Fortunate children have had parents and siblings who keep him involved in as much of *normal* life as the sensory deprivation allows.

The concrete topical constructs include colors, sizes, shapes, body parts, foods, clothing and toys. These are easy concepts to use for lesson plans in lipreading, sign language or auditory training. They are usable as constructs to emphasize the concepts. They are critical because they can call upon a multi-sensory approach. Thus, the senses of touch, smell, and taste can augment the vision in establishing the concepts. An example is the teaching of the concept of sweet and sour. Taste is employed in helping the eye grasp the idea of a *lemon* or to interpret the sign for lemon, while the ear (with amplification) is calling up the residual hearing to identify the sound.

Abstract topical constructs are more difficult. The topics of time relationship, citizenship, family relations, morality, and religion pose greater problems. A clock, for example, may be a secondary symbol relationship to time. Morality is an attitudinal entity and needs a wealth of referential experience.

Topical constructs are excluders. When one topic is chosen it automatically eliminates nonrelated vocabulary, sets the boundaries for probable visual clues, and rules out many stimuli which, regardless of sense modality, may otherwise be relevant.

Environmental Constructs. The environmental constructs are time, location, temperature, lighting, attire and appearance, and events. For example, it would be far less probable that a teacher taking a class to visit a farm would be giving a lesson on great musicians than a lesson on domestic animals. This illustrates both location and event constructs. Another example would be a costume. Should a clown in costume be brought into a school, it is most likely that this attire construct would direct the students to dwell on circus-related discussions.

Lighting plays a paramount role as a construct when vision is being used as an alternate communication modality. The amount and direction of light on the speaker's face are environmental constructs. Here we are using the term in a slightly different way than in the preceding paragraph. Here it refers to the situation and physical comfort of the student. It refers to the classroom facilities and to the object—space—element constructs. Physical and emotional discomfort can be negative effectors caused by environmental constructs. Perceptive teachers and children are aware of this fact, and, even though they do not discuss it, their actions may be evident to the experienced observer.

DISTRACTS

When the author resided on the family ranch he was involved in the care of horses' hoofs. When the horse was *unhappy* with what was being done he became quite restless. The experienced farmhands then employed a type of nose twister which was effective in distracting the horse's attention without doing any harm to the animal. As the horse's greater concern was his nose, he paid less attention to the activities around his hoofs. This was the result of a priority claim. The concerns in effect are: 1) To which stimulus should I direct my attention; and 2) to which stimulus should I give a response. The answers lie in the priorities, in which stimuli will be ignored or given at least secondary attention, and in the selective avoidance of response to inappropriate or irrelevant stimuli.

Previous experience with specific or related stimuli help the individual select the ones to avoid. The hearing impaired subject may find this a more trying task than the normal hearing individual because he may have had fewer stimuli with which he has had experience. He may respond differently because of the distortion of the stimuli and may be utilizing clues which the normal hearer does not consider. Let us recall how many of us had great difficulty in hearing the verbal communication of the astronauts during the early space flights. We were very aware of the accompanying sounds but had to learn to ignore them, as did the communication experts in the space centers.

The ruling out or avoidance of distracts is a prime consideration. Distracts are of the same general categories as constructs. Anything that takes away from the critical stimulus is a distract. In some cases, things may be distracts until the stimuli become meaningful. On the other hand, they are distracts because they already are meaningful. Auditory distracts are of the greatest concern in dealing with the acoustically handicapped. These individuals begin the entire communication process with the constant presence of distorted or missings sounds. These are distracts. Or, with amplification, the non-stimulus sounds may be exaggerated sufficiently to be distracts. Naturally, the lack of previous experience with specific sounds are, in many ways, distracts. All other senses can also be the receivers of distracts. They bring in the distracts of object—space—element discomforts of other stimuli which may seek priority of attention. Nearly anything which takes attention away from pertinent stimuli can be considered a distract.

Disturbed emotions and psychological problems are distracts. We can also include the emotional and psychological entities of the parents and other associates.

Many of the emotional and psychological distracts of the deaf stem from the manner in which other people have reacted toward them. The parents may exhibit many types of responses when informed that they have a deaf child. If these responses are adverse, they become distracts that capture the energies which should be spent on proper treatment of the child. The parent's concern over his/her guilt, fear, humiliation, or rejection of the child and/or deafness are distracts. This parent has inadvertently chosen a destructive priority. The child is the loser.

The deafened individual has many distracts because the problems brought about by an adventitious deafness cause a need to reassess his potentials. He faces the probability of changes in employment, society and recreation. The mentally healthy person is able to live through these transitory distracts. They can be of too great a concern during the period in which he should be primarily involved in various other facts of aural rehabilitation. As he works through these programs they become constructs which assist in guiding him.

The deafened individual has the distract of close associates rejecting him as being personably less desirable. This is a distract because he must convince these rejectors that he is still a human being and has all other faculties intact.

Priorities must be assigned and all associates must help in this process. The constructs then take on perspective, the distracts take on less significance, and the development of aural habilitation results.

MONITORS

A deaf person must recognize whether or not he understands the constructs. He needs to know if he has the right constructs, is using them correctly, and if he has given proper priorities and has ignored the distracts. Two mechanisms are involved: the servo-monitors and extereo-monitors.

A common illustration of a servo-monitor is the thermostat found in the family home. When a member of the household has set the temperature control at the desired level, the properly functioning heating system keeps the room temperature within the prescribed limit. Should the room temperature fall below the prescribed variance, the mechanism triggers the motor switches that permit the system to increase the heat. Then, as the heat rises, the procedure is reversed, and the mechanism is *shut down* when the temperature reaches the maximum variable limit.

Human servo-mechanisms go beyond that of a machine because they create their own levels and their own permitted variables. Aural habilitation helps establish these levels, as does the child's entire developmental environment. The child learns what will be tolerated, what gives him pleasure, and what he will accept as an accomplishment. He gets feedback from his senses and from emotions which guide his next activity.

When there is a disturbance in a sense modality, there is a disturbance of the servo- monitor. This is demonstrated by one test routinely used in the audiological evaluation of suspected cases of pseudo-hypoacusis. The Lombard test is based on the voice-reflex phenomenon. The person with adequate hearing speaks more loudly in the presence of noise. On the contrary, the deaf person has a malfunctioning servo-monitor and has to depend on other methods of controlling his speech. It is a basic fact that *we talk the way we hear.* Aural habilitation incorporates the development of the *normal* servo-monitors or the training of others to compensate for the defects. This problem is compounded when there are multiple handicaps.

Organisms respond to their environment. All nature is somewhat symbiotic. The living plant or animal modifies and is modified by its effect on other things. When an animal of prey hunts it has some idea how the quarry will respond. Then, as the victim of the hunt moves, the hunter does likewise. The reverse action-reaction roles of the two are also in effect. Those responses are extero-monitors.

The same principles apply to communication. Some writers discuss this in terms of activity-reaction; others present it as conditional response. The point is that subject A modifies or continues his activities on the basis of the activities of subject B. Subject A uses the responses of subject B as extero-monitors of the effectiveness of his own efforts.

Together the servo- and extero-monitors inform the individual if his constructs have been correct and properly used. They inform him if he has given correct priorities to the stimuli.

CHAPTER 5

AUDITORY TRAINING –
LANGUAGE DEVELOPMENT

M ANY BELIEVE THAT at the time of birth it is irrelevant whether the child is deaf or has normal hearing. During the following days and weeks sounds come from the infant in the form of reflexive and instinctive exclamations. The infant then starts to play with those sounds. He utters all the sounds needed for most of the languages of the world and tries them all. Gradually he notices that when certain sounds are uttered, certain things happen. The accidental use of specific sounds becomes deliberate when the child finds that he can control his environment by consistent use of the vocal outputs. The cry of hunger or discomfort is a native tool which is used to influence his parents. When the infant has accidentally used a sound repeatedly and received the same response each time, his brain establishes the relationship between sound and result. Inner language has begun on a subconscious level. The more frequent and consistent the utterance-response experience the more firmly it becomes established. There is random experimentation with other sounds. As they, too, have consistent responses they are incorporated into the child's prevocabulary. When sounds do not result in identifiable responses they are discontinued.

During the selection of these early alternatives, an equally important counterpart is taking place. Parents are auditorily stimulating the infant with a variety of sounds by conversation, speaking directly to the child, and singing lullabies. He is also exposed to the background sounds in the environment. Bells, bangs, rattles, rustling, and other environmental sounds are received. *Baby sounds* are spoken by the parent who may be unaware that by so doing he is enticing the infant to make the same pre–speech sounds. Parents combine these sounds with tactile and visual cues such as tickling or smiling. Multi-sensory stimuli are being used to elicit speech sounds, or other sense modalities are being used to enhance or augment the hearing.

Simultaneously with the pre-speech sounds, the child is becoming aware of speech *per se*. By this is meant real words. Children are exposed to thousands of hours of sounds, and the same words hundreds of times, before it is expected that their speech becomes identifiable and effective. Speech to which these infants are exposed is more than sounds but the manner in which they are used—the inflections, pitch, rate, volume and other emotional projection they carry, but also the intellectual messages they convey. Parents, grandparents, baby sitters and others capitalize on these facets of speech as they engage in vocal play with the neophite. As older people obtain the desired responses from the child, they progress to the use of words to obtain the same reaction. It is important that this child have this auditory stimulation. The child is being bombarded not only with sound but also with experiences. Sound and experience become one, and this process is then refined. Stimuli and responses become concepts, and concepts beget other concepts. Concepts become the ingredients of communication, and communication becomes the framework of life.

As a culture we have established limits for normal development. Normal development presupposes normal functioning of our senses. When there is normal input through these senses there is supposedly no interference that would prevent refinement of all the activities we deem essential to living in our society. Poor mental or emotional health can prevent this normal progression, only tangentially, even when all senses are intact.

The acoustically handicapped is deprived of one sense. Unless the habilitation team is called upon, the individual has little chance of approaching normal. The communication framework for life can become a faulty structure. Communication ability may be lacking or distorted, and the experience with sound is distressing, either receptively or expressively. With the totally deaf there is an experiential vacuum with sound. For them it is as if sound does not exist. They do not know of such an entity by experience.

With the hard of hearing and deafened there is an experiential distortion or imperfection. During the developmental stages they are asked to interpret sound they can only accept as existing in spite of their never having experienced it. The deaf are asked to interpret segments of sounds and distorted sounds as efficiently as the normal. They also must live with frustration and even humiliation. These attitudes further deprive the deaf of experiential growth.

With the passing of a few months, the inborn *talent* of experimenting with vocal output of the hearing handicapped is observed and deliberately rewarded more specifically than it would without the awareness of hearing loss. By doing so, the parent substitutes other rewards for the absent hearing feedback. Rewards breed repeated attempts and tell the child that *something he is doing with his voice* is altering his environment, even if he does not actually hear it or hears it in a distorted manner. The child's attention is directed to visual cues and cues through other senses. A total habilitation program is in progress.

CONCEPT DEVELOPMENT

Auditory exposure and related experience give birth to concepts. It is difficult to state which comes first—receptive, expressive or inner language; probably they cannot be completely isolated, but the pivotal point is inner language. Inner language is a concept comprehension. As the stimuli come into the brain, there is first an awareness of the presence of something. Sounds make their presence known in the auditory cortex. At first there may be bewilderment, fear of the unknown, resentment of the invasion by the sound, or curiosity. Cortical and subcortical circuits find some relevancy in the sound. There is the attempt to determine if that sound has ever been heard before and, if so, what it meant. The first time it reaches the brain centers there is an attempt to relate the sound to other similar sounds, the meanings of which are already known. The process taking place is generalizing. As incoming sound and meaning are combined, concept develops. As concept develops, we have what we call "inner speech development."

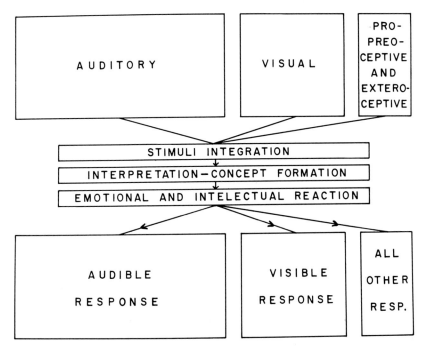

Figure 2. Communication in the normal hearing person has the major input by the auditory sense modality with secondary input by the visual, proprioceptive, and exteroceptive modalities. The cortex integrates these stimuli and the result is interpretation and concept formation. Then, the emotional and intellectual reactions are expressed in audible, visible, and other responses.

In the hearing impaired the percentage of the auditory-audible and visual-visible is reversed. The extent of reversal is dictated by the severity of the hearing deficit.

Inner speech development is not only related to incoming stimuli, as the child is making his own sounds. Whether he hears or develops concepts as his sounds cause consistent results. The concepts of output and reward establish themselves.

Communication specialists discuss the validity of an individual having inner speech while having some deficits in receptive and/or expressive language. Aphasiologists who have worked with both agnosias and apraxias can verify that there can be residual inner language despite the other losses of function. Therefore, it seems logical that the same can be true on the developmental level.

A university professor asks if you can think without words. Class members will be quite vehement in stating yes or no. An interesting follow-up statement is: "Alright, then think in some exotic language." By all probability (depending on the rarity of the langauge), the student will declare that he cannot because he does not know the words. The logical follow-up conclusion is, then, we cannot think without words. Only the more perceptive will ask for the definition of *words*. What are our definitions of speech and language since we are involved in aural habilitation. Speech is a mutually understood oral and visual code, and language is a standardized, mutually understood, use of that code.

The sounds and visual cues take on meaning, become concepts, and thus have import to the life. All the subtleties in the use of this code add impact. The more intelligent person can employ the code more effectively and improve his language. Intellect allows measuring the capacity of the inner language to reason on abstract levels. The hearing impaired begin their thinking on a concrete level. As concepts compound concepts, inner speech and language move into the abstract. The level of abstract ability is, in turn, the measure of language.

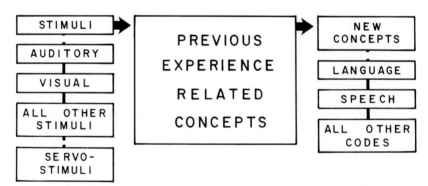

Figure 3. Concept formation originates from the interaction of stimuli with previously grasped concepts and previously related experiences. The new concepts are then expressed through language, speech and other codes. With the hearing impaired, there is usually a deficit of experiences and concepts because of previously restricted stimulus input.

Now let us consider expressive speech development. The members of the aural habilitation team who consider the deaf person's speech, i.e. pitch, loudness, and quality as the ultimate measure of development are misinformed, ignorant or pathologically myopic on a pet priority. Speech is only a means toward educational, social and emotional development. The latter are what should be measured. One wonders how speech can be developed to increase its role in reaching maturity.

The sounds of speech should be made accessible to the auditorily deprived, even if it is in a distorted manner. The profoundly deaf infant discontinues his own pre-speech because he hears neither his own nor that of others. He is urged to repeat the sounds he does hear. Without understanding, the parroting of sounds causes identifiable results, and he uses the sound again. The imperfect hearing compels the teacher to use visual, tactile and kinesthetic cues. The cues become related to the child's utterances. The creativeness and originality of the teacher limit the cues presented. When sophisticated cues are correctly interpreted, sophisticated speech will be the end result. A multitude of signs and symbols depict pitch, rhythm, inflections, tempo, loudness, phrasing and grouping, voicing, timbre and momentum. Each of these should be both a concentrated and ongoing facet of speech training, and are critical concepts to be grasped.

EXPRESSIVE SPEECH RETENTION

The deafened have known and heard speech. The basic speech and language components were once an integral part of their lives, and abstract levels of language were evident by inflections, quality and other elements of workaday speech. While they were still hearing their own and other voices, their servo— and extero—monitors kept them cognizant of the values of *elite*—sounding speech. Their hearing resulted in constant adjustment of their speech and maintained a purity of speech. When the hearing is lost, be it gradual or sudden, the monitoring stops. Frequently it has been observed that within one year of loss of hearing a person's speech becomes distorted or unintelligible where there are no substitutions for the aural monitors.

Fortunately, children and adults can learn alternate monitoring procedures. Loss of auditory feedback should not necessarily result in deterioration of speech. Awareness of kinesthetic sensitivity becomes finer, and awareness of facial expressions is enhanced. Residual hearing receives sound via amplification. Emotional involvement may be either beneficial or detrimental to the speech retention programs.

If an extended time has passed since the onset of the hearing deficit, all the techniques and procedures applicable to speech and language development for the deaf are appropriate.

Auditory training and concept development should begin with daily exposure to sounds; they should never end. They are omnipresent needs, and there can be no ultimate perfection. Total aural habilitation is a goal.

CHAPTER 6

ORAL EDUCATION OF THE HEARING
IMPAIRED (LIPREADING)

D EPENDING ON THE SCHOOL of thought, lipreading is a substitute for hearing and is considered an adjunct to auditory methods, or an enemy to be conquered. We all do lipreading to some extent but are unaware of it until someone makes a statement like, "I can't hear you. Wait until I put on my glasses." Usually this emphasizes the role vision plays in our workaday world.

Lipreading has been called visual hearing, cued speech and speech reading. It is the observance of movements of the lips, face, body and accompanying gestures that are part of aural communication. The *pure* oralist feels that the use of gestures should not be included. He feels that incorporating any gestures is a distraction and an enemy of the oralist's school of thought. The oralist limits his association with other hearing impaired, often to the extent of denying the similarity of sensory deprivation. He may become adamant against any incorporation of manual communication, claiming that sign language is a deterrent to functional communication.

The primary argument oralists use in defense of their school of thought is that the deaf must live in a hearing world, therefore, they must learn to use only those tools that are routine and standard in this environment. They maintain that speech reading can convey all the nuances of aural communication that are essential in the worlds of society, commerce and industry. They feel that the orally oriented individual is more easily and readily integrated into these worlds. Dependence on manual methods, they feel, limits the number of persons with whom they can talk. Data from several research projects support these contentions.

41

Some of the early expounders felt that lipreading was the appropriate approach but that the learner would become able to read only the lips of his instructors. They also believed that the deaf did have the capacity to learn receptive language. Others were more adventurous and included the teaching of speech in their educational programs.

The *conservative* oralists permit some restricted usage of manual communication in specific or unique situations. They observe that some times and places are not conducive to a strictly oral technique. They will permit some use of signing when the oral approach is clearly failing to transmit the messages. In many schools for the deaf in England, the limited employment of manualism has been used for years. This philosophy is applied in most American schools that have a *total approach*.

Conservative oralists feel free to use gestures in conversation, noting that this is a natural phenomenon in most cultures today. One quote states, "Tie a Frenchman's hands and he can't say a word." Not only the Frenchman is guilty of this. Note, for example, how many people use gestures while talking on the telephone. It may look absurd to an observer but, even though the listener on the other end of the line cannot see it, the gesturing helps the speaker become emotionally involved in the message and be more effective in his intellectual and emotional projection via the telephone. Conservative oralists are aware of this fact and consider it part of normal life.

Conservative oralists are inclined to restrict their circle of acquaintances to other deaf persons of their own orientation. They, on occasion, will show hostility toward other groups, including the pure oralists. They associate with hard of hearing, if that is their extent of sensory deficit; or with the profoundly deaf, if they have a more extensive loss.

The third group is the *liberal* oralists. These people are basically secure within themselves. They are not threatened by other orientations. They do not feel they are making any compromise by using the manual approach.

Liberal oralists maintain that children should be given every available opportunity to be educated in an oral school. As for themselves, they may or may not have acquired a usable knowledge of finger spelling for communicating with the manualists. Should they have this knowledge, they resort to it when the oral medium breaks down.

The liberal oralist is more willing to associate with any other deaf group. They do not categorize as readily as do the other oralists. They consider each hearing impaired as an individual.

The latter group of oralists will employ interpreters realistically, as indicated by their needs and communication limitations. They will manipulate the interpreters not to defend their own identity, but as a basic right used with any kind of professional service.

In the midst of controversies over oralism, there are basic considerations concerning the development of lipreading skills. Ewing and Ewing believe there are three stages in the development of speech reading. They are:

1. Obtainance and utilization of the child's natural glances toward the face of the speaker.
2. The interpretation of language.
3. The association of words with meanings without additional guidance.

In discussion of the first stage, the profoundly deaf may not give natural glances to the face of the speaker, particularly in cases of the congenitally impaired. It becomes *natural* only if from infancy he had been oriented to it. On the other hand, it may be noted that all animals get basic cues from the heads of both friend and foe. Some people may claim that is a protective instinct of the lower forms of animals, and others may feel that it is taught by the parent animal. The natural tendency to localize and turn toward the source of a sound (in the case of speech it is the head) is absent in the congenitally deaf. They cannot turn toward something that. their sense mechanism does not tell them exists.

As for the second Ewings' steps, it may be a case of semantics as to what their definition of *language* is. There is no language until a symbol has meaning. The observed movements of the lips and face are associated or equated with some experience before the symbol has meaning. The writer feels that a more appropriate phrasing would be *integration into language*. None of the movements of the lips transmit messages until those movements are identified and associated with specific logical and/or emotional parts of the lip reader's life. In the larger aspect, the second stage is that the deaf child begins to integrate the lip movement symbols with the aid of constructs and the use of other senses.

The last step is the child's functioning on the level of comprehending lip movements as words with meanings (both denotative and connotative) without the assistance of backup systems. When this is achieved the individual is an experienced and proficient lip reader.

Speech reading may or may not be treated as a classroom subject for the deaf. There are discussions of the techniques, procedures and methods; then practice is stressed, but with children it may not be a part of the curriculum as is writing, geography, and history.

For maximum benefit, lipreading should begin in the preschool years and be used continually throughout life. Like the manual approach, the oral school is as much an atmosphere or attitude as it is a method. Basic training in military service centers on personal establishment of attitudes of, *we can win,* togetherness, acceptance of experienced authority, and self value within the unit. All of these military attitudes are applicable to speech reading. The parents of deaf children may inadvertently instill attitudes adverse to the development of lipreading skills. They seek counsel upon which approach they should use, and are bombarded by proponents of opposing methods. They become confused and close-minded out of self-defense. Other parents may be influenced by the emotional involvement of those from whom they seek help, resulting in a bewilderment that is projected to the child and which the child interprets in the parents as *maybe there is no way you will ever use speech*. Fortunately, most parents are strong enough to rationally select one course or the other.

Attitudes are not only limited to children and parents. Our aging population faces the same problems. At first, some senior citizens will claim that they have no need to lip read, but that everyone else should speak better; others will seek means of learning the art. The latter are more numerous and, by the time they come to the training sessions, most are highly motivated and find it an enjoyment leading to success in their venture.

Along with attitude there must be the supposition that the lipreading trainer has adequate visual acuity. The deaf—blind or the blind—deaf are not candidates for lipreading; this is not to say that the partially sighted do not benefit from the gross movements of the face and lips. These visual cues may be valuable, particularly in subjects with profound hearing losses.

With the dual handicap of impaired hearing and impaired vision, people capitalize on the use of residual vision just as all aural habilitation must employ all residual hearing. Imperfect vision negates the possibility of developing fine discrimination and specific lipreading training, and realistic goals must be established in the training program.

Creation of a special language for the deaf child is not recommended. If one were developed, it would only have to be discarded later on as the developing child will need to abandon it in favor of the language used by his environment at large. All parents recall some of the terms our children use within the family circle, especially during the formative years, and how there was confusion when the term was not understood outside the family. With the deaf child this transition could be even more traumatic, because they do not have the normal hearing and vision that makes the change easier.

The rate of training should be governed by the child's ability to identify and differentiate the units (movements, positions, etc.) of lipreading, the visual and auditory memory spans, the facility to incorporate new materials into everyday use and the rate of learning permitted as a function of mental capacity. As with normals, deaf children are individual in their speed of comprehension and learning.

Consider the specific lipreading training experiences and casual language together. During the more advanced and sophisticated sessions of lipreading training, the emphasis is on specific lipreading. Training will be effective only to the extent that it is an outgrowth of general lipreading with associated experiences related to casually spoken language. Similarly, the specific lipreading is accomplished as the symbols read become concepts by their relationship to experiences. A purist in logic may maintain that the lip reader is not actually reading until experience makes the movement or position of the articulation into symbols holding meaning. As the lipreading of specific cues are put into the larger context of casual spoken language, the lip reader finds himself becoming proficient.

The goal of speech reading training is the ability to grasp the ideas transmitted by the speaker. Therefore, it is logical that from the beginning the central theme of each training session is the lipreading of ideas. In most schools of thought, single words do not make good lipreading material because ideas are seldom transmitted by only one word, and failure to put a word into the construct of a sentence increases the probability of error in interpretation. This is particularly true of homophonus words. For example, take the word [raIT]. Consider *right* or wrong, *right* or left, *right* of way, *Wright* (family name), *rite* (as a religious service), *right* (in civil courts), and *right* (as to get it correct).

The sequencing of language training as a part of learning lipreading is questioned. There is no significant data supporting a sequence different from that used in language training of the normal hearing pupil. Current emphasis and concern centers on language development. Many language specialists begin with nouns of identification and the placing of names on the objects in the child's world. Next comes basic verbs and then adjectives, numbers, prepositions, pronouns and conjunctions. Other teachers may vary this sequence, but not substantially. Frequently, forms of *to have* and *to be* are difficult. Verb tenses are rather abstract, and even the normal hearing have difficulty with these. Refinement of verb form is essential to a comprehensive and sophisticated language. The totalist's schol of thought has recognized the necessity for refinement and has devised a more specific signing for these troublesome verbs.

Seldom do we talk directly face-to-face or hold our head still when talking. Because of these facts, lipreading lessons and practice are more nearly the same as the *real world* when different facial angles are stressed. One deaf teacher of the deaf prefers to read lips from a 100° angle. He finds less distortion and less distracts in the presence of persons who try to make themselves more lip readable.

It is particularly valuable to use objects rather than pictures when working with two to three year old children. Pictures are less effective because they are, in actuality, abstract. Pictures lack the third dimension, texture, true size and opportunity to view from different perspectives. Handling of objects is a critical factor in normal development, as can be seen when a child's adventurous hands reach out to anything in sight.

During this two to three year span, the child is apt to be independent and prefer to work alone. By the age of four or five, the social self is awakening, and he will enjoy working in groups of two or three. This preference helps impress upon him his need to lip read other people than his family. He may go through a period of depression with feelings of failure when he tries to expand his circle of friends, and he has difficulty comprehending their speech. The teacher should be aware of these problems and help the child overcome them by capitalizing on the socializing nature when it is at its highest level.

If the child has had good experiences by the time he is of kindergarten or school age, his orientation toward oral communication will be well established. His environment has guided him through numerous listening experiences, and many contexts have been used. Constructs, be they sequential, topical or environmental, have become automatic considerations. The child has developed an ability to disregard many distracts. Teaching of the school subject can be the goal for the day.

In the older hearing impaired, an effective approach is to view lipreading as a hobby rather than as an arduous task. The attitude is a powerful factor helping to form and shape motivation, just as motivation helps form and shape attitude. Students of lipreading make the best progress when working with a relaxed state of mind.

Both synthetic and analytic approaches to speech reading are successful with patients. Some make better progress with one method than the other, and possibly the best approach is an eclectic one. In training programs where a total approach is the preferred orientation, each teacher is free to use either a synthetic or an analytic method in concert with manual cues.

With satisfactory visual communication as the goal, regardless of the approach, concepts are carried by the spoken word. Both the analytic and synthetic methods are concerned with transmitting and receiving concepts, yet they view them from different perspectives. The synthetic starts with the larger constructs and focuses on the message. This school establishes the setting within which lipreading is done. The outside boundaries are established. The student then has general concepts within which he finds specifics. The emphasis is not so much on lipreading all individual lip and face movements.

Distracts are influential considerations with both techniques because both have distracts unique to their approaches. Where the presentation of two similar words which look alike are distracts to one technique, this may be a plus value to the other. Teachers also find that children will be more affected by some distracts than others.

In regard to the monitors, note that knowledge of successful lipreading is the greatest monitor of all. Ultimately, it comes down to a visceral experience, that *feeling of confidence,* or either a sophisticated or elementary plane.

Some guides to follow in teaching lipreading are to create and maintain an environment in which speech is a significant, pleasant and successful method of communication. Visual cues are combined with the residual auditory perception and the tactile and kinesthetic modalities. With discretion, improper articulation is corrected, voice quality and speech patterns are likewise altered, giving no reinforcement by accepting poor speech and encouraging spontaneity of speech and lipreading.

CHAPTER 7

MANUAL EDUCATION OF THE DEAF

M OST TOTALISTS AGREE that lipreading is an effective method of listening. The pure oralists maintain that any hint of manualism is to be avoided and that manualism is an unnatural entity restricting communicators to only those who know manual methods and interfering with development of other facets of speech communication. In certain contexts, all of these are viable claims if manualism is interpreted in the ultimate degree to the same extent as pure oralism. There are rare cases, however, of manualists failing to encourage speech reading as a companion to sign language.

Perhaps the ideal concept could be for pure oralists and those few pure manualists to accept the reality of the total approach which would benefit all the auditory deprived.

Manual communication can be considered as having two parts —finger spelling and signing. Finger spelling has a specific configuration and/or movement of the hand for each letter and number of the language. It is designed to give a hint of the orthographic symbol. A little imagination is a valuable asset during the hours of learning the alphabet symbols. Even the untrained will recognize some symbols including o, c, l, and z. The designers of the signs considered common gestures, sizes and shapes, functions, and activities. Gestures are rarely used without finger spelling. Just as with spoken language, signing has some symbols that have different meanings. The use of finger spelling helps give clarity. For example, the signs for *winter* and *cold* are the same. Either one or the other would be spelled if they existed in the same sentence. In situations where lipreading is also observed, it eliminates the confusion of which interpretation should be chosen.

Idiomatic expressions, regional dialects, and idiosyncrasies exist in manual communication as they do in the spoken word. The

Figure 4-A. Manual communication is closely related to the gestures, body, and facial expressions. A) Minimal visualization is needed to see the similarity of the hand alphabet and the orthographic alphabet. The *K* is a prime example.

customs, industries, and communication habits of a community create special needs for special signs. Signs can mean various things in various geographic areas. The inconsistency of the language must be pointed out to the manualist.

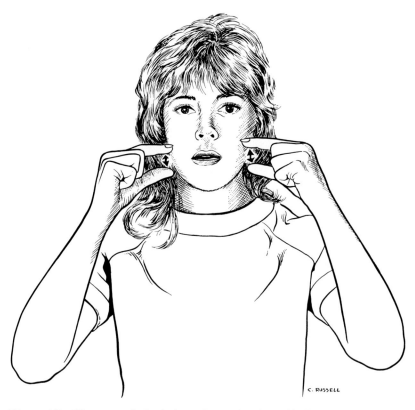

Figure 4-B. The manual depicting of "gossip" is easily interpreted and remembered because of its relationship to the mouth movement.

Manual communication is not a static language, and it is constantly being enlarged, updated, and refined. A major emphasis in the last few years has been on detailed specific signing of the tenses of the *to be* verb. The refinements are easily read by the experienced manualist and are readily understood by the novice. This refinement eliminates the basis for the statement of the oralists that sign langu-

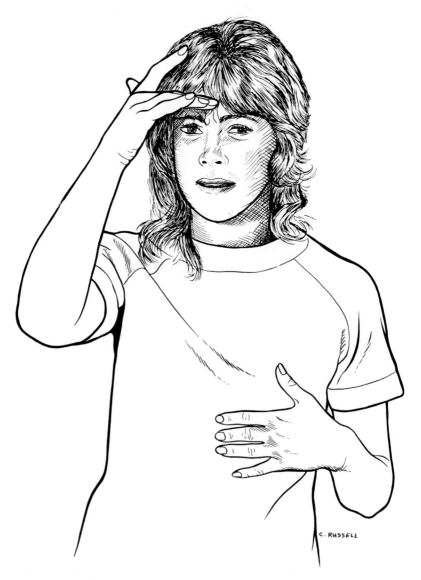

Figure 4-C. Facial expression is an integral part of manual communication, illustrated by the expression of pain on the face, while the signer is pointing to the head and stomach.

age hinders lipreading by being different in grammatical structure.

It has been said that manualism takes shortcuts. This is true but no more than the shortcuts we take in our daily conversation. Everyone uses phrases rather than complete sentences or words instead of phrases. The oralists should recognize that these shortcuts also complicate the problem for the students in their schools of thought.

When idiomatic expressions are part of the communication, manualists may use either substitute signs or words to convey the literal meaning. Since idiomatic expressions are a major part of our language, development has been largely through formal classroom training rather than incidental hearing.

The interpreter may translate the idioms literally, paraphrase them and perhaps even explain them. Idioms are concepts. We transmit concepts of ideology, philosophy, religion, and interpersonal relationships such as sarcasm and humor by idiomatic expressions. The concepts, by the time they reach the idiomatic stage, are abstract and have to be analyzed before they can be interperted.

The beginning manualist soon learns that sign language, too, has sophisticated and complex idiom-like expressions which are difficult to translate to the nonmanualist world.

Manualists, primarily interpreters, give consideration to the educational level of the sign reader. The more highly educated prefer verbatim translations with the interpretation being left to them.

Various verbal levels of the deaf determine the use of idiomatic expressions and employment of concrete or abstract terminology. This is true with either the oral or manual method. Some deaf are low-verbal or non-verbal with regard to the functional level. They cannot make themselves understood without an interpreter, nor can they understand without an interpreter. Language disability coexists with the low-verbal deaf. The orally trained depend on a few words they can lip read, and the manually trained are limited to a few signs. For these individuals, the more concrete the signs the better.

Fortunately, most deaf function on a conceptual level. They work with concept images. Some writers call these mental images which develop into words. Manualism helps convert concepts into words. As sophistication develops, there are more subleties in the signing and the signs have more complex meanings.

The deaf of higher intellectual and socioeconomic strata rely less on the use of signs and use more finger spelling. This frees the person from the limitations of standardized signs and allows him to use all the vocabulary of the hearing world.

A rich experiential background, with a basic conceptual background, lessens the possibility of a nonverbal or low-verbal deaf child. A child does not become nonverbal or low-verbal because of his being manually oriented; rather, manualism is used because it is an effective means of communication.

The use of slang can be considered with either regional dialects and colloquilisms or with idiomatic expressions. Frequently slang is difficult to translate into sign language because it is unrelated to the signs used in the training programs and in practical situations. Some persons may consider slang as being abstract symbols. However, analysis of slang verifies that it is a substitute for indepth thinking, and the words used have no relevancy to the discussion. Some interpreters recommend that the slang not be interpreted for the deaf because of its lack of value other than to show that the speaker either has strong feelings or uses slang as an excuse not to show his/her true, strong feelings.

Manualists, on the other hand, have their own slang which is translated into oral language only with difficulty and loss of impact. The verbal deaf, especially those with higher educational status, ignore and avoid slang.

With sign language, one uses analogies, parallelisms, rephrasing, or paraphrasing. For example, in Thespian skills facial gymnastics are used. Signing demands an alertness using alternate visible symbols, as lipreading demands that alternate words and phrases be used. As the manualist observes the responses of his reader, his exteromonitors inform him of the reader's comprehension with the conceptual background. Experienced public speakers, businessmen and educators, and backyard conversationalists rely on assorted terminology. Therefore, the manualists who do likewise should be encouraged. Manualists call upon the specific backgrounds and interests.

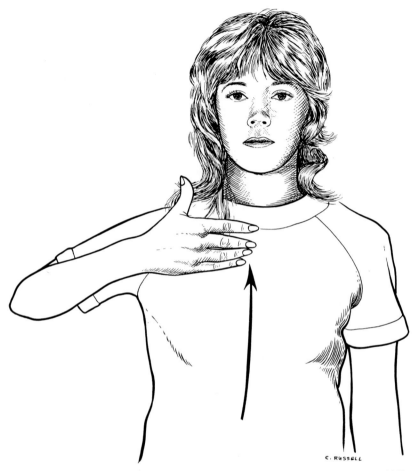

Figure 4-D. Visceral experiences are considered in some signs. The middle finger is brushed upwards against the chest for the word "feel" just as we frequently say "my stomach was in my throat."

When a person is first oriented to the manual school, it is well to practice on the low-verbal level. There is a void of sign knowledge, experience, and conceptual framework. By beginning on the low-verbal level, concrete rather than abstract facets are emphasized, and they become a solid foundation for forthcoming growth. This approach puts thought into its simplest English forms, using words with a common meaning.

There are some specific situations where manualism or manual interpretation are significant. First, consider a courtroom in which the facilities for lipreading are not optimum. The oralist will lose much as he turns his attention from one part of the courtroom to another, searching for the speaker. The interpreter or manualist does not have this problem. The legal terminology is also different from the deaf's usual vocabulary, making it difficult to lip read. Much confusion can be eliminated if there is a pretrial orientation with the lawyers and the judge. There should be agreement on ground rules as to the procedure for manual interpretation. The deaf are not frequently found in courts, but when they are they should be entitled to every constitutional right extended to the normal hearing.

The very dignity and stature of the deaf may be challenged when ignorance on the part of others in the courtroom cause impatience and misunderstanding. The deaf person does not have the knowledge of courtroom routine and may appear unimpressed without the assistance of an interpreter. When the auditory defect is explained, his participation is more complete. The use of a manual interpreter lessens the possibility that the deaf person will be accused of using his hearing loss as a means of evading the issues.

In a medical environment, there are distinctive vocabularies and concepts. The case histories, with presentation of symptoms, and the questions come easier with an interpreter because it lessens the possibility of misinformation, misdiagnosis and incorrect therapy. In this reference, we can point out the problem and accompanying frustration in trying to lip read such unfamiliar language as abscess, belch, constipation or wheeze. The interpreter can simplify terms such as amputation, biopsy, cautarize or wet dressings, particularly with low-verbal patients. This accomplishment calls for imagination and ingenuity.

Only the experienced medical interpreter can feel the need for strong support between himself and the patient. There must be no suspicion that the doctor and the interpreter are discussing the patient in secret, without full translation. Rapport helps the patient understand that the routine distractions of a doctor's office are not related to him.

Manual communication during counseling the deaf may have primarily the same psychological mental and emotional problems as the normal individual. The *total* habilitation counselor is cognisant of this fact. Paranoia is also a common psychological problem of the deafened. They want to be able to expend themselves, and sign language serves a dual purpose. It serves as their language code and a means of emotional discharge. Recently, a deaf woman, who had been orally educated through the junior year of high school, related the burden that was lifted from her and her associates when manualism was incorporated into their communicative skills.

There is the need for confidence to be religiously maintained with an interpreter. Objectivity is necessary because of the nature of the communication. The interpreter should be an inanimate transmitter of messages in both directions without personal bias, logic or judgment. He interprets without condemnation or approval.

Psychology for the deaf is rapidly changing. It is a very concept-oriented science on an abstract level, and it is difficult to establish satisfactory signs for the manualist. Finger spelling is the major mode for the individual. Low-verbal deaf, in particular, are at a disadvantage in counseling sessions.

Next, let us consider the sign language as an approach to religion. Regardless of the affiliation, we should agree that discussions of a *Supreme Being* and our relationship to it are of an ethereal rather than tangible basis. Each religion has some *tangeable* objects to help relate to the Almighty. With Christianity there is the cross and the nail prints in the hands of Christ. With other Christian faiths there is a peculiar garb or ritual that lends well to manual speaking.

When sign language is used and interpreter is needed, it is better if he is of the same faith. This is not so much for fear that someone of another faith will inadvertently cause an incorrect interpretation, but it is because a person of the same faith is acquainted with its subtle variations.

One should avoid uninterpreted conversations and the use of friends as personal interpreters, except in direct interaction between therapist and patient.

The total school of thought seeks the use of residual hearing. Hearing aids and/or auditory trainers are utilized. Background, warning and other environmental sounds are important to the totalist. Residual audition is an adjunct to sign language, and sign language is an adjunct to residual audition. Residual hearing lipreading, and manual communication comprise the total approach.

CHAPTER 8

MOTIVATIONAL AURAL HABILITATION

THE AURAL HABILITATOR should inform the hearing impaired of his deficiencies and that there are things he does not know or does not understand as he should. In training programs, the personal expectations serve as a goal. To have motivational aural habilitation, teachers should design specific objectives and help the student in attainment of these objectives, thereby, satisfying both his wants and needs.

The first goal in aural habilitation is the understanding of the handicap. In the deafened, this can be done with a direct approach. The teachers of the older deafened individual can use logic in descriptions and explanation. The deaf should be informed that there are no mental or emotional anomalies associated with the hearing deficit. Neonates must be given love and assurance.

The hard of hearing are instructed as to which sounds they do not hear or hear in a distorted manner. They are informed that there are some sounds they may never hear. Some readily understand that other sense modalities will be employed in compensatory ways. The young use these alternate senses involuntarily, and then are informed what has been taking place.

Identification of the problem and the restrictions regarding communication are significant. Identification is the key and the precursor to understanding, acceptance and correction of the defect.

Teachers should evaluate the trainee in three ways. One, he should be tested on the same measuring devices used for normal hearing subjects. Secondly, he should be evaluated with others of similar hearing ability. Thirdly, and perhaps most importantly, his own goals and abilities which are determined through psychological and aptitude testing should be evaluated. With these one can evaluate the progress. Both children and adults are more willing to participate when they understand a technique or procedure.

UNDERSTANDING OF PROBLEM BY ASSOCIATES

Each patient is part of a group. He has parents, siblings, playmates, teachers, and other associates. There is a relationship that has to be understood by each member.

Parents, siblings, and other members are to understand the hearing ability, the goals and objectives, and the techniques and procedures to be used. They should be instructed in normal and abnormal development, and they must understand the psychological and emotional complexities that the patient endures. Most of all, they must understand their reactions to the auditory loss and to the people with these losses.

Audiologists or teachers of the deaf must face family members who exhibit fear, guilt, and hostility toward the affliction or the afflicted. The professional should clarify the nature of the involvement and emphasize that negative attitudes and willful ignorance are antagonists. Unwillingness to learn destroys acceptance of potential, techniques, and procedures, and it makes it impossible for that person to play a dynamic role on the habilitation team.

The external motivation of the auditorily deprived comes from the parents and spouse. Acknowledgment of the presence of the deafness, determination of its affects, and concentration on compensatory avenues of communication are all necessary.

All members must be instructed in the educational expectations, noting that with children there will probably be a one to two year developmental delay. One cannot equate hearing loss with cortical deficiency. Associates should realize that the deafened take a little longer but *can* generally arrive at a satisfactory educational level, at least through the secondary training. Associates are more responsible for educational loss by the deaf than the deaf themselves.

The associates are to be instructed in occupational potentials. Any job which does not require acute hearing as a prerequisite should be available. The National Technical Institute for the Deaf, in Rochester, New York, recently has stressed the wide variety of possibilities. Sources of financing for training available to the

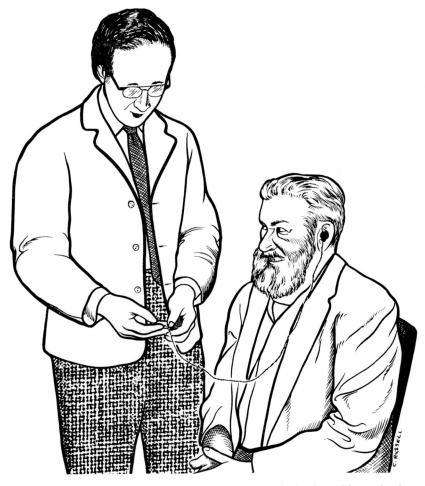

Figure 5. Aural rehabilitation of the aged commonly begins with a selection of a suitable hearing aid. Important considerations are: correct response curves and gain of the aid, understanding of the limitations of the aid, psychological acceptance of the adjustment to its use, and instruction or orientation in utilizing the instrument.

parents should be investigated.

The patient's associates discover his/her social potential, and the various schools of thought dictate the social milieu. Each school of thought has its rationale and methods for approaching *normal* social existence.

PSYCHOLOGICAL COUNSELING OF THE HEARING IMPAIRED

A young boy sits at the edge of the field; he has been excluded from the football game as he could not hear the signals. He may not know that this is the reason, and may feel inadequate. He needs psychological counseling with encouragement as part of the rehabilitation.

A young mother who is gradually losing her hearing wonders why her children no longer bring home stories from kindergarten. She feels frigid isolation developing and needs emotional help.

A senior citizen notices that his friends and family no longer stop to chat as they had in the past. There is loneliness, and, again, there is need for psychological counseling.

These situations illustrate the loneliness, isolation, and solitary life associated with hearing loss. The deaf need support and assurance that somebody cares for them.

Other problems also haunt the deaf, such as: 1) Why did this happen to me? and 2) What am I doing to others because of my handicap? The question that surpasses all others is: Why do people treat me the way they do? This is not paranoia, it is a sincere emotional response.

The deaf must accept the isolation associated with a hearing loss. Psychological counselors assist by giving instruction on how to minimize the deficit. They teach alternatives by changing the attitudes of others. The deaf must also help themselves by educating others.

These people want compassion; they do not want pity. Compassion is acceptance, tolerance, and assistance. Compassion is also understanding and comprehension. Compassion is not an equivalent of approval.

The auditorily deprived must learn compassion for the hearing world who do not understand. Psychological counselors instruct the deaf in the compassionate form of life. The deaf have difficulty in understanding the lack of acceptance and wonder why others consider them odd, unique, and undesirable. Gradually they learn that ignorance is the mental-emotional orientation of these rejectors rather than compassion.

The acoustically impaired must realize that their auditory limitation does place a burden on others. Until this consideration becomes an important ingredient in the counseling, there is danger of egocentricity developing. The properly-instructed deaf know how to encourage the hearing world to modify its usual code.

The deaf realize that less consideration is given them beyond the family circle. A busy store, a crowded bus or train, or a sporting event are designed for the normal hearing, and the deaf cannot expect the environment to accommodate them. They must apply themselves to fit into society.

Psychological counseling, in preparation for society, is routine in schools for deaf children; but for the deafened of advanced years, the social circle will either stabilize or become smaller. The counseling emphasizes that the deafened can become isolated unless they are motivated toward socialization.

Thus, psychological counseling is an integral part of occupational and vocational guidance. Counselors should emphasize the potentials, stressing that the characteristics of the hearing loss are directionalizing limits and are not restrictions. If an adventitious hearing loss forces a person to change his occupation, vocational counselors should utilize such information. With help, the deafened can look forward to happy, prosperous, productive, and gratifying livelihoods.

PSYCHOLOGICAL COUNSELING OF THE ASSOCIATES

It is better for the child to have parents overcome the period of grief and unacceptance than it is for the parents to continue refusing to admit that a hearing loss exists.

The parents tend to be introspective. Psychological counselors may help them, and members of the clergy should also be oriented for assistance during this time of personal need. Guilt involves morality. Parents seek pastoral help and become depressed when it is not forthcoming. Counseling of this nature is not constructive to the welfare of the child.

The auditorily deprived need love, and it should be the key in early counseling. He/she needs all the care and tenderness of a normal child. Parents are guided into the demontsrative affection given to the non-impaired. Equality with siblings begets love from the siblings. Grandparents, too, are a source of emotional, affectionate support. Adjustment is easier for the mother than for the father, but counseling should be considered for both parents.

All concerned must realize that there are limitations of educational, vocational, and other goals. The counseling sessions lead the parents through the stages of acceptance, alternatives, planning, and striving for appropriate goals.

An additional thought on counseling is the importance of a sense of humor. If both the hard of hearing and normal associates are able to see the lighter side of life, if they can interpret thoughts, words and actions with the normal ingredient of levity, and if they can laugh with each other and at the deficit, there is some assurance that a degree of emotional and mental health will be maintained. Humor is considered a catalyst and a savior.

CHAPTER 9

EDUCATIONAL PLACEMENT

I F A DEAF CHILD IS ABLE to receive an education in a normal environment, the hearing impaired has a negligible effect. There are sufficient compensatory modallities to minimize the hearing loss; they may be in the form of electronic amplification and/or visual cues. Education begins with the recognition that a hearing loss exists.

In the home and school, the child learns the interpersonal dynamics of his/her life. Schools for parents may be more than contacts with other parents who have shared the experience. Associates of parents help them realize that what they are doing is correct; they know they are sharing responsibilities, fears, anxieties, hostilities, and frustrations.

Informal parental groups are probably in the lesser populated areas, where homes with deaf children are more distant. In the densely populated area, it is economically feasible to establish formal programs. Note that the percentage of deaf does not change, only the overall number. Hearing societies, college and university clinics, United Fund agencies, and public instruction districts may have ongoing training for parents. Many programs insist that the parents be an integral part of the children's training. Some groups schedule sessions to permit the father's involvement.

In addition to the local parental guidance groups, the John Tracy Clinic, in Los Angeles, California, has a correspondence course available to parents of the deaf, and it has international participation. The course can be used separately or in conjunction with other programs. Content of the lessons ranges from mental and emotional considerations to family relationship and helping the child prepare for life in society.

Schooling for the acoustically handicapped child includes pre-

Figure 6. Group parent counseling permits the sharing of adverse feelings and concerns with other parents under experienced guidance. Feelings may include mourning, fear, hostility, bewilderment, and unrealistic hopes.

school clinics. Day programs take the child on a part-time basis with the goal of helping the child learn that hearing and speech are essential, useful, and enjoyable. They help the deaf children learn to relate to other children. Parents learn to relate to other children, may participate with their children and/or other children, and are instructed in carryover techniques and procedures to make the home, school, or clinic extensions of one another. There are a few centers that have resident facilities for children under five years of age, but they are for special cases with extenuating circumstances.

During the preschool years the parents must choose between oral, manual, or total communication. They are bombarded with all degrees of propaganda, ranging from the dogmatic promulgations of the pure oralist to the *confirmed* manualist. In larger metropolitan areas, both approaches are available. In the lesser populated areas, only one or the other may be available.

Among the criteria for selection let us consider the extent of the hearing impairment. The more severe the deficit, the more totally the child must rely on the visual sense. Some children have an intellectual and emotional makeup that will tolerate the rigor and frustrations of oral education. These children have a different synthesizing ability than those who are better trained by total methods. Parents help in the development of these abilities during the preschool years, but a professional teacher of the deaf may note subtle manifestations of preference of the alternatives which the parental training cannot alter. The child may enjoy and appreciate the fine differences of clues. His/her attention and interest span may favor the oral or total symbols. Most important, the child may grasp concepts more readily by one method or the other. He/she may be more comfortable and successful in attempts at communication, oral or total, and may incorporate more *good* speech with one of them. Effectiveness of transmission of concepts, grammatical construction and evidence of rational thinking are the goals. At times oralists are surprised when they notice the effectiveness of total communication compared with manualism.

One of the major considerations in the selection of the oral or total school is the psychological and emotional makeup of the child. Each child has individuality with a means of coping with reality, fantasy, anger, and frustration. Children have a threshold of tolerance and a level of emotional tension under which they function best and a level beyond which they cease to make any effort. One child may be best served by the oral approach, while another will succeed with the total. If the child is *unsuccessful* in one school, he should be referred to the other. The training of a child in pure oralism may isolate him/her from intellectual and emotional growth related to exposure to other deaf who may have experienced types of growth which the pure oralists has not.

If the hearing loss is borderline, the auditory therapist can integrate special sessions with the classroom subjects. The therapist can instruct the child on how to receive maximum benefit from his/her residual hearing and the utilization of visual clues.

Selecting seating, with the better ear closer to the teacher, is recommended. The teacher should realize the need for his/her face to be visible and be aware of the need for optimum lighting in the room. The teacher should give attention to communication among the students and accomplish it unobtrusively without calling attention to the hearing problem.

Those children needing special attention are placed in a special classroom where they are given the major part of their education, but is incorporated into specified classes where the hearing deficit does not interfere or where help is received which is not available in the special classroom. Sports, laboratories, and shops are in this category. The special classroom is usually housed on the campus with the regular classes, but occasionally students are bussed a considerable distance.

In day schools, all of the education is done by teachers of the deaf and the students are usually profoundly deaf. They are in either the oral or total communication programs, and may have contact only during the school hours with normal hearing children.

Figure 7. Tactile and kinesthetic sense modalities can be effectively used as a means of helping the child differentiate between voiced and voiceless cognate speech sounds. Several hearing handicapped have stated that they believe this is the third dimension of speech.

Many children begin the primary grades in full time programs; they then progress to integrated programs. The more verbal they become the more they can communicate and the better they are prepared for the integrated school system. Parents may have the misconception that once a child is in a full time program for the deaf he will remain there for the balance of the school years. However, schools for the deaf have the aim of integrating the children into the hearing world at large, and progress of the children govern the integration.

Not all children receive maximum benefit from day school programs. It is regretable that the home and family are ill suited as a domicile for the deaf child. Perhaps the adverse situation is economic. Perhaps there are other handicapped persons in the family, or it may be that interpersonal dynamics between parents or among other family members indicate that the child would be better off away from home. Counselors must face these realities frequently.

The deaf child may be sent to a residential school for the deaf when other facilities to help the child are not available. Such is usually the case in rural areas.

Multiple handicapped children may need special schools. As an example, the child may be a deaf-blind, blind-deaf, or deaf-cerebral palsy child.

For advanced education, more and more community and senior colleges are establishing programs for the deaf. The most advanced training facilities for deaf adults are at the National Technical Institute for the Deaf, in Rochester, New York, and Gallaudet College, in Washington, D.C. Both of these facilities have been federally assisted from their inception, and Gallaudet extends the education through the Master's Degree level.

There are numerous facilities through which vocational rehabilitation agencies work, such as the Veterans Administration. Selection of hearing aids, teaching lipreading and sign language, and extensive counseling are deemed as necessary on-the-job training. Some agencies also furnish the aids, ear molds, and batteries; others are influential only in the selection of the proper aid.

As a rule, aural training of the older deaf takes the form of hearing orientation, lipreading, sign language, and counseling. In some instances, it is more helpful to relatives and associates. Motivation for participation in these golden year activities varies. A positive motivation is the desire to maintain communication with loved ones. A negative factor is the resentment of the invasion of sound into their silent worlds.

Hearing societies, some university speech and hearing clinics, and senior citizen clubs provide these services. The members of an aural habilitation team should be knowledgeable of the available services to whom reference can be made.

Any handicap may leave a family with monetary deficits, and the expense of hearing aids and accessories may be considerable. Residential school generally assess charges for room and board, and expect the clothing and grooming expenses be cared for in the same manner as if the child were at home.

State and federal funds are often available for both school and post-school needs. Hearing societies are United Fund agencies, usually charging a minimal clerical fee. Senior citizen clubs vary in their financial structure. Private schools, including those under the auspices of churches and religious fraternal orders, charge on a cost basis. Regardless of cost, education is an inherent right of the hearing impaired and the privileged responsibility of all.

CHAPTER 10

REEVALUATION

THE AURAL HABILITATION TEAM evaluates the hearing function, the behavior and level of development, and potential of the child or adult. Various members of the team have select responsibilities, but the entire design is not complete until all the responsibilities have been filled.

Usually evaluation begins with the parents' recognition of the problem. The first step is the evaluation of the child's reactions and responses to measurable sounds, usually pure tones. Test data establish the starting point for all other procedures. The data should be used for comparison by repeats of the test, and monitoring any change during the habilitation process.

Aural habilitation can be considered a research procedure because we begin and end by ascertaining thresholds. Air conduction testing is to be repeated by earphones and by sound field presentations. There is the possibility that, with first testing of infants, one of these procedures was not done prior to the training program. At monitoring points and at the conclusion of the program, speech tests are readministered. Most pediatric audiologists have had children on whom they could not obtain consistent intitial speech test results because of the low-verbal level existing before training. Obtaining significant speech test results at conclusion of a training period is, of itself, evidence of partial success.

The speech tests for discrimination, sentences, speech in noise, and differentiation among sounds comprise a total audiologic evaluation and are to be included. These tests are important in evaluating the success of auditory training. The period of time between evaluation and reevaluation may be shorter in the aged than with the child or youth, but the data are still pertinent factors.

The number and types of tests that should be conducted with

Figure 8-A and B. Play audiometry is adequate for most children to co-operate in the audiological evaluation. Classical conditioning is pertinent because the child gets a reward when presented with auditory stimuli. The audiologist is alerted to any consistent response. Games and procedures appropriate to the age of the child are selected.

amplification are controversial. Overtesting is preferable to under-testing.

SPEECH REEVALUATION

Training programs for speech and hearing personnel have a core curriculum course in voice and articulation. The students learn the four classifications of articulation disorders, and are trained to identify voice anomalies such as poor quality, improper pitch or volume, disorders of rhythm and rate, and unsuitable inflection and stress. Articulation is measured against the norm of the geographic area in which the subject lives. The articulation should not deviate from the norm, in order to be distinctive, and it is a subjective judgment. The determination of appropriate voice quality, pitch, volume and rate is even more subjective. It is more difficult to record data on the latter qualities during the initial evaluation, and much more difficult to compare at the time of reevaluation. High fidelty recording is the best means for documenting the data. A two- track recording system records the pre- and post-training vocal output and facilities ease of comparison.

LANGUAGE REEVALUATION

Language structure facilitates communication; and in language reevaluation, the common language is our criteria. Diagnostic tests and devices are used as the measuring tools; they ascertain the overall language levels including the consistencies of the written and spoken word, the linguistic picture, and the vocabulary.

In comprehensive re-diagnosis the nonverbal language is evaluated. Gestures, body language and facial expression all play a part in the total language concept. Manual communication is considered either verbal or nonverbal. Fluency, accuracy, and consistency after training also need evaluation. The effectiveness of the entire communication process is reexamined.

One should evaluate how abstractly the hearing impaired can reason and communicate after aural habilitation; also, how they grasp and use concepts, and how completely they employ closure in mental processes. If the education program has developed the talent to express themselves clearly to people of assorted mental, chronological, and educational levels, the language function is satisfactory.

EDUCATIONAL REEVALUATION

Achievement tests indicate the success of the educational process, and the child is ranked with a peer group. The hearing impaired is confronted with an additional measurement, the output performance. It is not measured against peers but against that of the normal individual of the same age.

Educators of the deaf base their interpretations of test data on past experiences. Findings indicate that the education of the deaf is about two years behind that of normal hearing students. Oralists and totalists maintain that their individual approaches, techniques, and procedures are more effective in attaining the optimum educational level. Each school of thought is engaged in post-training evaluation. Statisticians and researchers agree that the testing device partially preordains the findings, with the district director in which the child is educated dictating the tests to be administered.

Followup interest and preference tests are also administered. Additional educational training can alter the interests, and open new doors. With falure to reevaluate by interest and preferences, the hearing impaired are stereotyped and unlikely to advance.

Curriculum committees have the perennial problem of deciding the requirements for a well-rounded liberal arts training. The progressive parochial educational system recommends the harmonious development of the physical, mental and spiritual values; others believe that education is not complete unless aesthetic interests are stimulated. Creative and performing arts should be encouraged. It is the opinion that the habilitation team should evaluate the effect of training in aesthetics for all hearing impaired.

EMOTIONAL AND PSYCHOLOGICAL REEVALUATION

Formal and informal psychological evaluations are conducted with the battery of tests attempting to determine the adjustment to the hearing deficit. The person must accept the fact of a sensory deprivation and its accompanying limitations but utilize education, social and occupational alternatives. The reevaluation may indicate that a person has not developed his/her assets, or it may point out that the ambitions are totally unattainable. In either event, it indicates that there is still need for further emotional and psychological adjustment.

Post-rehabilitation psychometrics have revealed that the deafened frequently are plagued with latent paronia.

One of the intermediate indicators of successful psychological adjustment is the patients' acceptance and understanding of amplification as a substitute, poor though it is, for normal hearing.

Other post-training tests indicate the person's self-image, body image, willingness to compete with the man on the street, comprehension of his/her place in society, and religious health. There are endeavors to find causes for self-imposed seclusion. All of these portray one's psychological identity.

There should occasionally be psychological reevaluation on

other members of the family to determine if the parents, for example, have survived their periods of mourning and guilt and accepted their roles in the entire process to a point where they are of help rather than a hindrance. They must realize that they are offering most assistance by cooperating with others on the team.

Some of these evaluations do not have standardized tests. The psychometrist must resort to a visceral reaction for data. Hearing deprivations are very personal matters, and further research will provide still more evaluation tools.

VOCATIONAL REEVALUATION

A feeling of accomplishment and independence are two basic needs of a human being. Vocational training programs are designed to meet these requirements. A sense of initial achievement is a motivation toward greater achievement. Success, accomplishment, and esteem are of equal value to the hearing impaired. Success is a companion as well as a parent of self-esteem, and an improved self-image breeds further achievement.

In our society, everyone is expected to contribute to its preservation and improvement. Aural habilitation programs train people to make this contribution. The individual's potential and strength are evaluated and a *contributing role* is selected as probably the most suitable one for the individual. The training progresses, but after the patient has finished his prescribed curriculum and is employed, we need to reevaluate.

The reevaluation or post-training evaluation is concerned with optimum use of talents, happiness with employment, being in an occupation where a hearing deficit does not place one in any type of danger, and opportunities for advancement.

FINIS

Many reevaluations have answers that defy standardization in the true scientific sense. Members of the habilitation team must remember that they are working with human beings. All questions for reevaluation can be answered, but the answers cannot be treated merely as data; they are the communication extensions of human lives.

BIBLIOGRAPHY

Berg, F. S., and Fletcher, S. G.: The Hard of Hearing Child and Educational Audiology. *Proceedings of International Conference on Oral Education of the Deaf.* Washington, The Volta Bureau, 1967, pp. 874-885.

Binnie, L., and Alpiner, J. G.: A Comparative Investigation of Analytic vs. Synthetic Methodologies in Lipreading Training. Paper read at American Speech and Hearing Convention, Chicago, 1969.

Canfield, Norton: *Hearing: A Handbook for Laymen.* New York, Doubleday, 1959.

Calvert, D. R., Reddell, R. C., Donaldson, R. J., and Pew, G. L.: "A Comparison of Auditory Amplifiers for the Deaf. *Exceptional Children, 31:* 247-253, 1965.

Dale, D. M. C.: *Applied Audiology for Children,* 2nd ed. Springfield, Thomas, 1968.

Davis, H.: *Hearing and Deafness.* New York, Rinehart, 1947.

Elliot, L. L.: Descriptive analysis of audiometric and psychometric scores of students at a school for the deaf. *Journal of Speech and Hearing Research, 10:*21-40, 1967.

Elliot, L. L., and Armbruster, V. B.: Some possible effects of the delay of early treatment of deafness. *Journal of Speech and Hearing Research, 10:*209-224, 1967.

Fisher, B.: An investigation of binaural hearing aids. *Journal of Laryngology and Otology, 78:*658-668, 1964.

Gaeth, J. H.: Learning with visual and audiovisual presentations. In *Deafness in Childhood,* McConnell, F., and Ward, P. H. (Eds.): Nashville, Vanderbilt, 1967.

Hartbauer, R. E.: *An Introduction to Your Child Who Has a Hearing Impairment.* Loma Linda University, Loma Linda, 1967.

High, W., Fairbanks, G., and Glorig, A.: A scale for self-assessment of hearing handicap. *Journal of Speech and Hearing Disorders, 29:*237-264, 1964.

Hirsh, I. J.: Use of amplification in educating deaf children. *American Annals of the Deaf, 113:*1076-1055, 1968.

Hirsch, I. J.: Auditory training. *Hearing and Deafness,* 3rd ed. In Davis, H., and Silverman, R. S. (Eds.).

Hoverstein, G. and J. Keaster: *Suggestions to the Parents of a Hard of Hearing Child,* American Academy of Opthalmology and Otolaryngology, 1959.

If You Have a Deaf Child, Urbana, University of Illinois, 1949.

Lenneberg, E. H.: *Prerequisites for Language Acquisition. Proceedings of the International Conference on Oral Education of the Deaf, 113:*283-294, 1967b.

Matkin, N. D., and Olsen, W. O.: Induction loop amplification systems: classroom performance. *ASHA, 12:*239-244, 1970.

Mindel, Eugene D. and Vernon, McKay: *They Grow in Silence,* National Association of the Deaf, Silver Springs, Maryland, 1971.

Montgomery, G. W. G.: Analysis of pure-tone audiometric responses in relation to speech development in the profoundly deaf. *Journal of the Acoustical Society of America, 41*:53-59, 1967.

Myklebust, H. R.: *The Psychology of Deafness,* 2nd ed. New York, Grune and Stratton, 1964.

Myklebust, H. R.: *Your Deaf Child: A Guide for Parents,* Springfield, Thomas, 1950.

O'Neill, J. J., and Oyer, H. J.: *Visual Communication for the Hard of Hearing.* Englewood Cliffs, Prentice-Hall, 1961.

Oyer, H. J.: *Auditory Communication for the Hard of Hearing.* Englewood Cliffs, Prentice-Hall, 1966.

Pollack, D.: *Educational Audiology for the Limited Hearing Infant.* Springfield, Thomas, 1970.

Pollack, D., and Calvert, D. R.: *The Semantics of Deafness. Volta Review, 69*:644-649, 1967.

Tervoort, B.: Development of language and the critical period, in the young deaf child: identification and management, *Supplement, Acta Oto-Laryngologica, 206*:247-251, 1964.

U.S. Department of Health, Education and Welfare: Human communications: the public health aspects of hearing, language, and speech disorders. *NINDB Monograph* No. 7, 1968.

Watson, D. M.: *The use of Residual Hearing in the Education of Deaf Children.* Washington, The Volta Bureau, 1962.

Whetnall, E., and Fry, D. B.: *The Deaf Child,* Springfield, 1964.

INDEX